My Answer
by
Oswald Mosley

My Answer

Oswald Mosley

ISBN-13: 978-1-913176-15-0

Sanctuary Press Ltd
71-75 Shelton Street
Covent Garden
London
WC2H 9JQ

www.sanctuarypress.com
Email: info@sanctuarypress.com

"Is every politician who opposes a war during its progress of necessity a traitor? If so, Chatham was a traitor and Burke and Fox especially; and in later times Cobden and Bright and even Mr Chamberlain (Joseph), all these were traitors."

Lloyd George speaking at Oxford in 1900

Contents

Part 1 - Preface in Answer to a Home Secretary.   3

Part 2 - Essay In Foreword   11

Part 3 - Quotations   51

Part 4 - Statement written in Prison by Oswald Mosley   59

Tomorrow We Live   65

    Introduction   67

    System of Government - What is Wrong ?   69

    British Union System Of Government   77

    Economic System - What Is Wrong ?   97

    British Union Economic System   115

Part 1

Preface in Answer to a Home Secretary.

May I apologise for the necessity recently imposed upon me to begin this book with the trivial and absurd? That necessity arises characteristically and inevitably from the presence of the Labour Party in power. Readers of the "Essay in Foreword" which follows next in this volume, will observe that it was written some three months before this preface. That review of recent years contained some application of the method of analytical psychology to the mind and technique of the Labour Party. It was, therefore, a fortunate coincidence that, in the interval between the writing and the publication of this book, those entirely subconscious processes of mob psychology, which, in the Labour Party, are a substitute for thought, should have operated to provide a striking illustration of my theme.

My thesis in this connection was:-

(1)   that the Left are obsessed with the desire to suppress by any means an Idea which they fear because they cannot answer it in argument;

(2)   that they are accustomed to charge against others, with great sound and fury of moral indignation, very similar faults to those which were in evidence in the early history of their own Parties.

It was interesting, therefore, to note that the Home Secretary had this book very much in mind when making what members of his Party described, with premature delight, as a "startling exposure" in the House of Commons on June 6th, 1946. In a reference to me, he observed, "I can only hope this will be

an instructive foreword to the book he proposes to publish."
Unfortunately, the Foreword was already written for a more
serious public than the Home Secretary is accustomed to
address, but I respond readily to his courteous invitation by
writing this additional short preface on a matter which so
strongly supports my previous argument. The statement of
the Home Secretary assists me in relation to my first point,
because it cannot be held that the issue of this statement, in
response to the question of a supporter between the writing
and publication of this book, was exactly designed to secure
it a favourable reception. In fact, it might be held that some
such occurrence was the only method left to suppress an idea
in advance, by attempted discredit, when the two most widely
canvassed suggestions for eliminating that idea had already
been reluctantly discarded as inapplicable. These methods
were the introduction of special retro-active legislation and the
operation of obsolete Statutes. The difficulty of our opponents
in applying either method in pursuit of their ardently desired
objective of overcoming our idea, without facing an argument
to which they feel themselves inadequate, is analysed at length
in the following "Essay in Foreword."

The statement of the Home Secretary also assisted me in relation
to my second point, because he was accusing me of doing the
kind of thing in which a subsequently elected Leader of the
Labour Party appeared to have been mixed up years before, and
was attempting to place British Union in a position which bore
some points of similarity to a situation once occupied by the
Labour Party.

Our authority concerning the history of the Labour Party in this
matter was no less a figure in the story of that Movement than
the late Lord Snowden, who remained one of their outstanding
heroes until he decided in 1931 that the second Labour
Government, in which he was Chancellor of the Exchequer, was
too incompetent to continue.

Preface in Answer to a Home Secretary

The reader will find full detail of the controversy arising from the intervention of the Home Secretary in the House of Commons, between the writing and publication of this book, in the Press of June 7th, 1946 and in the "*Daily Herald*" of that date, in particular. Any interested person will find —

1. The Home Secretary's allegation that letters had been found from the Italian Ambassador in London, among Mussolini's papers, which purported to show that I had accepted funds from Italy on behalf of British Union in the years 1934 and 1935;

2. My categorical denial of this statement and dismissal of such evidence as worthless on the grounds that evidence on any subject could now be available at a penny a packet in alleged Italian archives if any ill-disposed person sought to damage me or deceive authority, together with my challenge to the Government to produce any serious evidence from Bank accounts, etc., to which they had long had full access. (It may here be added that it is not long since phrases about the "lie factories" of Europe were current and popular, while the discovery of "revealing documents" was made the subject of universal merriment: The hilarity of most people is but little diminished if the factories change hands. The self-evident absurdity of these "Letters" bears the same ingenuous hallmark as the recently "discovered" and published marriage lines of the German leader, which contained some elementary mistakes in the German language).

3. My quotation from Lord Snowden's Autobiography which cited a communiqué of Mr. Lloyd George's Government and attacked Mr. George Lansbury when he was editor of the "*Daily Herald*"; some years before he became the elected leader of the Parliamentary Labour Party;

4. The "*Daily Herald's*" refutation of Lord Snowden and denial of that Government communiqué as "untrue," together with

their statement that £75,000, in part composed of the sale of Russian Diamonds, had been "transferred" to one Director, but returned by him to the donors of the Communist International when the offer was made known to the other Directors, who unanimously decided not to accept it.

Far be it from me to intervene in this celestial conflict between the deceased Labour Leader, Lord Snowden, and the present "*Daily Herald*" which is elevated and gilded by the impeccable respectability of High Finance. But, in accepting the "*Daily Herald's*" account and rejecting that of Lord Snowden and Mr. Lloyd George's Government, we yet may note that the enterprising director, named by the "*Daily Herald*" recently stepped forth into a more genial sunshine of publicity when he received an honour on the recommendation of the present Labour Government. This charming and well-deserved tribute to his work in other spheres is only of interest to us here in affording some slight assistance when we measure with appropriate solemnity that high degree of moral indignation which moves the Labour Party at the very thought of any such transaction: Yet more moving, if a deeper emotion were possible, is the cry of the "*Daily Herald*" that "the story is over a quarter of a century old," which is a much shorter period in the life of the Labour Party than 12 years in the life of our Movement. So, even if the completely untrue had any measure of truth, we could yet seek solace with the lamenting "Herald" and murmur the poignant lines of Euripides — torn from a sadly different context— "Ah, youth and the days that were."

Now we understand that it was just a youthful indiscretion when the "*Daily Herald*" remarked in the heat of controversy with Mr. Lloyd George, "if we had accepted the offer of £75,000 from Russia, with which this Country has been technically at peace since 1855, though Mr. Lloyd George has starved and tortured its innocent women and children by his infamous blockade we should have done nothing dishonourable, and we should not be at all ashamed of ourselves. As it happens we have not accepted the offer."

Here we may leave this rigmarole of nonsense about funds on a small heap of damp squibs. The whole silly story of this attack upon us has been all too characteristic of the Labour Party when faced with an argument they cannot answer. We see again the old fuddled technique—on the one hand to represent us as a black and sinister menace rising in the very heart of Britain, and, on the other hand, to depict us as a phenomenon so absurdly un-English that we had no chance of success. Once again, let them answer themselves before we turn to serious things. We may leave this aspect of Labour propaganda to a remark dropped by their leading political journalist in a very frank moment, when past and present political manoeuvres were most remote. Mr Hannen Swaffer wrote in the *"World's Press News,"* on August 5th, 1943, under the engaging title "Mosley's Thugs Cowed," that "it was left to the War and 18b" and, in a further Paean of "Pink" thanksgiving, headed "Saved by the War" he added, "Yes, but for the war we might today have been a Fascist country." So the Party recipe for "International" salvation seems clear—when your system is bankrupt and you face self confessed defeat at home by fellow countrymen whose case you cannot answer— have a foreign War and suspend the centuries old British Law which preserves liberty, while you prate that you are fighting for liberty. So much for the suggestion that we were so un-English that we had no chance of success, which ever alternated with the concept that we were such an imminent danger to their system that special legislation had to be rushed through Parliament - vide the so-called Public Order Act of 1936, and Regulation 18b(1a) which scrapped British Liberty under cover of war, and the various special laws for which the "Left" still clamours.

In fact, the extraordinary results of our movement were achieved by the self-dedication and financial sacrifices of thousands of ordinary British people who carried on the work, and maintained the finances, of British Union's network of branches, which covered the country on an entirely self-supporting basis. Our headquarters was, also, financed by the sacrifices of individuals and, in this connection I have before me a Chartered Accountant's certificate, concerning the origin of our funds for a considerable period before the war, which shows each subscriber to be British. For this period we were able to obtain the permission of each subscriber to include their names; this was not always possible for the reason that, in the remote past, some people met ruin because they supported British Union, and more feared it. This certificate can be shown to any Chartered Accountant whom anyone cares to pay to examine it under professional pledge not to reveal the names of subscribers, or any detail beyond ascertaining that they were British. I have always refused to make a parade of my own sacrifices in the manner of politicians, but, as discussion of this matter has been forced upon me, it may be noted that this Chartered Accountant's certificate shows a contribution from me of some £24,000, which I reckon to be about one-quarter of my total gifts in support of my beliefs during my political life. In fact, in my case, the old platform crack had some validity to the effect that, whereas some Labour Leaders of the world entered politics poor and left them rich, I had entered politics rich and looked like leaving them poor. But let me hasten to reassure my anxious opponents that my gifts to political purposes were brought to an end by my entry into Brixton Gaol just in time to preserve my complete independence, because I still have quite enough left to save me from any temptation to be bought by anyone!

For the further comfort of my enemies let me add that the strictly commercial basis of my present activities, in these very early days, presents a most flourishing picture. I have long been convinced that the only really healthy basis on which to build an idea in this country is on the entirely self-supporting foundation of a business enterprise which is subject to the severest commercial tests. This Publishing House, so far, makes good progress under these tests which are unknown to any political party. In fact, we stand or fall by our own abilities — But — "in common humanity" — I must really cease to utter such subversive thoughts before the Labour Leaders have a heart attack!

For the rest of our discussion of past and current affairs and of the further reaching debate to come, is it too much to hope that the Labour Party can, at last, rise above the personal, the trivial and the merely silly to place principle against principle in a serious argument which is worthy of a great age of high decision? - June, 1946

Part 2

Essay In Foreword

My opponents have had their say; No-one, at any rate, will deny that! During years of enforced silence in gaol under Regulation 18B, and during a further long period under "House arrest," politicians and Press were free to abuse me to their hearts' content, without one word of reply. Men, who, before the war, had shown themselves very shy of responding to my repeated invitations to meet me in debate on the public platform, took full advantage of this opportunity for a one-sided controversy. Even after the end of the war and the emergency, which had been used as a reason for the suppression of our Movement and our policy, by the suspension of the effective provisions of the Habeus Corpus Act and every legal and traditional freedom many of them continued to agitate for a denial to me of any right even to publish my opinions. The mere suggestion that I might publish books produced a paroxysm of rage and hysteria, almost comparable with their fine frenzy at the end of 1943, when they demanded that I should be kept in gaol, without charge or trial, until I died, in face of an illness which, the doctors affirmed, would be fatal under those conditions.

The general claim to a right thus to assassinate, by mob demand, anyone whom these elements happen to dislike, probably also attracted the attention of others, in its full implication for the future. At the time I was past caring what they said or did; and this present brief review of personal experience serves merely to illustrate a tendency, then latent, which will inevitably assume a more open form, and wider application, as the political situation develops. Retrospect, without lesson for the future, is ever futile, and the sole purpose and justification of this whole survey of the past is to derive warning and direction for that future. However, whatever may be thought of the past, this new agitation to prevent me publishing books, or in any way expressing an opinion, is altogether welcome to me; for nothing could more clearly illustrate the main point which I have to prove. It is the idea which these people fear, and it was the idea which they always feared. They wanted us shut up during the war, not because we were "fifth columnists" or anything of the kind, but because they feared the spread of our opinions. No other suggestion of any seriousness was ever sustained. In particular, it was never, at any time, or in any way, suggested to us by the Government that we had broken any law. But by every kind of innuendo, if not direct statement, the public outside were led to believe that we might be traitors to our country at war, if we were at large.

It was, of course, impossible to prove any such suggestion to anyone informed of the facts, indeed it was a self-evident absurdity, if the facts and record in the matter were published, to suggest that we desired the defeat of our country, when for seven years before the war we had led the demand for its rearmament against any possible danger. In particular, such a contention would have come ludicrously from politicians who were then conducting the war, but, with few exceptions, had occupied themselves, prior to the war, in depriving Britain of the elementary means of self-defence, to say nothing of effective power to intervene in the remote quarrels which their policy was constantly demanding. (The magnitude and extent of the wars, which their policy required, were ever in inverse ratio to the means which these politicians were prepared to provide for their conduct).

It was thus easier for any conscientious objector of 1914 to become a posturing authority on military strategy in 1940 than publicly and openly to justify the retention of ex-servicemen in gaol, who had demanded national rearmament, while his Party refused even to permit cadets to drill.

So our whole affair was wrapped in mystery, by deliberate decision of every Party in Parliament, while arbitrary power tore up every vestige of the liberty for which it claimed we were fighting. Again and again from prison, I challenged the Government to publish anything they had to say against us and to permit me the right of a public reply; they were silent while the jackals were busy with the whispered lie. For all this I neither seek nor desire revenge; that emotion is the hallmark of small minds. Our opponents had their opportunity, and they ran true to form; that is all, and, as far as I am concerned, it is the end of that. So, in this matter, I deal only with Governments and Parties, and, in no case, with individuals. The part played by individuals within the system is of no interest to me; they merely carry out the policy which Governments and Parties create, with "collective responsibility"; and, once that policy is made, can do no other. I am not here concerned with men, but with the system which inevitably creates its types as well as its policies.

My motive in writing this book is the feeling that a man should bring to public judgment what he has said in the past before he speaks again, even if it be true that under this test most of our leading figures would be finally eliminated. So, in this book, writings are submitted with some confidence to the judgment of the British people, which were held to be so misguided or reprehensible during the war that the author, and some 800 of his friends, comprising over 85 per cent of the "18B internees" of British origin, were put in gaol or concentration camps, by a combination of all Parties, to prevent the further propagation of such opinion and the continuance of such activity. From this essay, in foreword, and the appended writings, anyone who is interested may obtain some conception of our mind and attitude at the time of our arrest; a subject which has been so long and violently discussed by the other side.

For those who are further interested to know what I think and feel, and what contribution I have to make, after the vast events which have since intervened, I am writing an entirely new book, which I hope will follow shortly.

My Answer

In the present book my fellow countrymen are asked to judge whether, in a land which claimed to be fighting for liberty, the Government was morally entitled to hold us in gaol or concentration camps under execrable conditions, whether, in the light of subsequent events, our opinions were proved right or wrong, whether they do not compare very favourably with the pre-war writings and speeches of many of our present rulers, whether these opinions, under the test of experience, do not entitle us to a better hearing, in the present and future, than our gaolers can claim in the light of the situation to which they have reduced this country and the world. But, 'before we come to this argument, I should deal with a doubt, which may still survive in some minds, as to whether the agitation for our imprisonment had any valid object other than the suppression of our opinion.

It has been stated again and again by Ministers in Parliament that we could not be charged with any offence because we had not broken the law. Our "detention" was described as "preventive", in case on any future occasion we should break the law. What were the grounds for apprehending this? Not our past record, for all of us, who were old enough at the time, had served in the previous war, and, between the wars, had been denounced as ultra-patriots demanding such unreasonable things as rearmament. It could not either be seriously contended that, in the light of our published policy, we were subordinate to any foreign movement. Our position in that matter had been very plainly defined in the foreword of the last work reprinted in the present volume, which had originally been published early in 1938. Any conception that we were so subordinate could only be sustained by the belief that everything we said was untrue and that my whole career had been a lie. To this the simple answer is that a man who had renounced so much, and passed through so many years of lone struggle, merely at the end to do the opposite of all the policies and principles he had ever proclaimed, was a case for a lunatic asylum rather than Brixton Prison. Whether this alternative was, in fact, more appropriate the readers of these pages must judge for themselves.

May I now be permitted to enquire why, in particular, the Labour Party find it so difficult to believe that anyone could hold the National Socialist or Fascist creed without betraying his country to movements abroad, which held foreign versions of that creed? Perhaps the explanation can be found in some speeches and writings of the early days of the Labour Party, during the would-be forgotten Socialist-Communist period, when, soon after the last war, a conflict appeared possible with the Soviet-Communist power of Russia. Subject to something of the same test between creed and country did the early Labour Party emerge so unscathed? Would all of them dare to republish their speeches and writings of that period, as I am now republishing my speeches and writings of our testing period in the last war?

For we were then subject to a test from which the English, in all the long strain of their history, had emerged always triumphant as we did. When England fought the Catholic Power of Spain, that event did not turn English Catholics into traitors; although it could be argued that, in a degree never present in any other case, they were subject to an influence whose centre of gravity was outside these Islands. Never did it cross the mind of a great ruler that Englishmen would succumb to such a test of character. On the contrary, leading Catholics, who happened also to be great sailors, were summoned to primary positions in the struggles of our early Fleet, which swept Spain from the Seas. What a contrast to the recent war when a retired Admiral, who had been Director of Naval Operations, and Chief of Naval Intelligence, was thrown, without charge or trial, for three and a half years into Brixton gaol, merely because before the war he had dared to advocate Anglo-German friendship.

But England, in the days of Elizabeth, knew not the debased passion of internal distrust, engendered by the alien mind of the new Money power in unholy alliance with international Socialism of the uneasy conscience. When the opposition of Charles James Fox and the Whigs to the Napoleonic Wars endangered the Government of Mr. Pitt, it did not occur to the latter, in the most violent heat of controversy, to accuse his opponents of being a "fifth column"; in those days some sense of honour subsisted between Englishmen. He knew that, if the French landed, the Whigs would fight for their country. Yet, when we stated our willingness to fight if the Germans landed in 1940, as we had fought in 1914, we were thrown into gaol.

In fact, only a tiny fragment of our previous associates succumbed to the test and proved disloyal; their number was infinitesimal in proportion to our membership. They rejected clear instructions on the outbreak of war, which are reprinted on page 40 of this volume, and followed the advice of a man who left Britain before the war began. He was expelled from our Movement as long ago as March, 1937, and attacked me and my friends for years before the war, during which he attacked this country. Against this insignificant handful can be set the thousands of British Union members who fought for their country, among whom many lost their lives fighting, with the last loyalty, in a war which they had deplored.

Those of us, who fought in the previous war of 1914-18, resolved to persuade our countrymen to make Peace, if we could, in a quarrel which seemed to us no concern of the British people; but, at the same time, to do nothing which could injure our country. In so doing, we were supported in our political activities by some younger men, who were devoted to the same ideal, and preferred imprisonment for their beliefs. As a man, who in one war knew fighting both in air and trench, and in the next war knew this country's gaols, I may, at least, be permitted to hold a very definite opinion as to which experience was the harder to endure.

Such was our answer to that supreme test of character when creed differs from the policy pursued by country, as expressed by a Government clearly supported by a majority of fellow countrymen. The response of the early Labour Party to that test can be studied in some speeches and writings after the previous war, when a fresh war with Socialist-Communist Russia loomed imminent: a little later, the Labour Party became, for the first time, the Government of the country. In contrast, our response to that test can be studied in the speeches and writings reprinted in this volume which led us to the gaols and concentration camps of "Democracy." (When the term "Democracy" is used in inverted commas, I do not mean what Democracy is in theory, but the thing to which it has now been reduced in practice).

There was never a moment's doubt as to our course on the one hand, to do nothing to weaken or injure our country for whose armament and strength, in a menacing world, we had ever striven; on the other hand, to do everything possible by the open political action, which the law then permitted, to persuade our fellow citizens first to keep the peace, and later to restore the peace. That course was dictated by the profoundest realities of nature which, in this case, are easily comprehended by any who begin to understand her deep laws. A man may not destroy his mother, however mistaken he may believe her to be. He may seek by every art of persuasion to restrain her from a dangerous folly. But, if she persists in that course, he may not join with her enemies to destroy her; on the contrary, he must, if necessary, defend her, however wrong, or even wicked, he may think her conduct. Anyone, who does not understand this, is incapable of grasping the profound and divine laws which govern that small portion of the universe which is discernible by man. It was no doubt a lack of that deep understanding which led an infinitesimal percentage of our former supporters to a course which violated that principle. As noted above, Socialists, who study certain utterances after the last war, during the Russian crisis, may search their consciences as to whether no larger proportion of their ranks failed to grasp this first principle. The present "Left" may further search, with some anxiety, for an answer to the question how substantial a proportion of their members will prove equal to the same test, if another crisis arises in Anglo-Soviet relations!

But politics are complicated matters, and still more complex and deep-rooted are the philosophies which underlie them; contrary to the current belief that they are the one subject which everyone can understand, with less attention than he gives to selecting his favourite brand of cigarettes. So, may we attempt to reduce the deep principle just discussed to a simple analogy which might arise in everyday life?; even if the suggestion of its occurrence in individual cases might create domestic difficulty. Supposing, a man's old mother expresses her firm intention to go down in fighting mood to the local, where a number of tough characters are wont to assemble. He will be alarmed: particularly if his old mother expresses her equally firm intention of slapping "that person's" face, if he does anything of which she disapproves. He may, in fact, foresee a packet of trouble; and his disquietude will be in no way lessened by the fact that his old mother has seen fit to arm herself for the occasion with nothing more formidable than an umbrella and a shrill tongue. But his course of conduct is perfectly clear. He will do his utmost to dissuade her from an undertaking which he feels can bring no good to her or to the family as a whole; if he fails he will not absent himself, but will accompany her. When the inevitable row begins he will do his utmost (1) to protect her, and (2) to extricate her as soon as possible with the minimum possible hurt. Any other course would be contrary to nature and every normal feeling of man. What an appalling conception that the son should be the first, when trouble begins, to stab his old mother in the back. No matter what his opinion of her behaviour, such action from him is inconceivable.

Yet this is precisely the conduct of which our opponents suggested we might be guilty, if left at large during a war which we believed to be a profound mistake. It matters not, for the sake of this argument, whether we were right, or wrong in our opinion; that question will be discussed later. It matters not, in this simple analogy, whether the son's view of his mother's behaviour was in any way valid. All that matters is the acceptance of the principle that, rightly or wrongly, he may profoundly disapprove of her conduct, and yet be inhibited by every law of nature, and every normal feeling, from raising a hand against her, or doing anything except succour and protect her in her difficulty, whatever its origin. He will seek to dissuade her— Yes—But he will never seek to injure her. Such was our attitude to our country in the last war. The reader may, or may not, think it utterly mistaken, for the moment that does not matter—but it is, at any rate, a position which he will understand and accept as honourable.

The acceptance of this simple principle, which is in accord with the whole previous experience of British history and character, shatters the vile and silly suggestion that, in seeking to dissuade our country from war, we sought her downfall. How did a concept arise which was so utterly alien to our national character?; a concept completely foreign to our every experience and tradition, whatever the experience of the Continent. We must revert to the question whether, since the war of 1914-18, the possibility has arisen for the first time that some Englishmen, in some circumstances, might feel the pull of foreign allegiance, in the event of a clash between Britain and Soviet Russia. For the origin of that suspicion let us seek not only in the speeches and writings of some Socialists, in the crisis with Russia after the previous war, but also in the sharp about-turn of the Communists, in the recent war, when Russia changed sides. It was easy for the latter to entertain such suspicions when their whole policy, even in recent times, had plainly been inspired as much by the vagaries of a foreign Power's policy as by the interests of the land which had afforded all of them hospitality and some of them birth; But the Labour Movement, by now, should have grown beyond these elementary and crude suspicions, born of the early "indiscretions" of their own Party (if we may employ an euphemism in the case of a Party whose own thin skin ever provides a striking contrast with the coarse and brutal jibes they aim at their opponents).

Perhaps a factor was operating in this matter which is well-known to psychologists. The Labour Party had a sense of "guilt," derived from the early associations with Russian interests of certain elements within their Party. Even if the people had forgotten those Socialist performances after the 1914-18 war, the Labour Party had not forgotten them. Some of them may even have re-read, in recent times, the pages of Lord Snowden's bitter references to those occasions in his Autobiography. Again, as the psychologists well know, a sense of guilt in oneself leads to accusations against others. Particularly, is a man disposed to discern in others a fault which he feels sub-consciously to be his own. With what vigour some parents, for instance, correct their own pet foibles in their children.

So the Labour Party, in fact, denounced, in our young Movement, the offence which had been discernible in the early days of their own Movement. The "guilt" of Labour in those days was visited on us. For, be it noted, the agitation for our imprisonment and, in the case of the extreme section, even for our legalised assassination, came ever from the "Left."

The "Right" had certainly no solicitude for us, and was glad enough to give a knock, when occasion arose, to people who had rendered more effective opposition to certain vested interests than the Labour Party, which, by its whole psychology and structure, was ever doomed to ineffectiveness in the ultimate analysis. But the "Right" scarcely made a show of believing the crude and absurd suggestions made against us and were frequently denounced for their indifference by the "Left," The fault of the "Right" was acquiescence in, rather than commission of, an offence against fellow-countrymen, whom they knew perfectly well to be innocent, not only in act but in intent. They could not engender the heat of the "Left" in this matter, however much they disliked us. For they were free of the "guilt" sensation of the "Left," in that, with all its faults, no elements in the movement of the "Right" had ever, at any time, substituted the interests of a foreign power for those of their country. On the other hand, within the memory of all who were adult at the end of the 1914-18 war, elements of the "Left" had exposed themselves to such a charge, and the "guilt" sensation inherited by the Labour Party from that period still survives, even after the comforting reassurances afforded by the soothing years of long-sought "respectability," which was achieved at last round Tory Dinner Tables.

But perhaps it is an error to diagnose, in psychological terms, so crude a phenomenon of a transient but inevitable historic phase as the Labour Party. Simpler to state that the "Left," in general, had an opponent down, by blow of Fate rather than their own exertions, and it was a good chance to jump on him! Their courage and roughness on such an occasion was, of course, in fair proportion to the frights he had given them on previous occasions! Above all, what an opportunity for the protagonists of "free speech" who were engaged in fighting a world war in that "sacred" name, to deny free speech to all whose opinions they really feared. Again, in passing, we may note a psychology which always accuses others of a crime which is inherent in their own sense of guilt. For the pursuit of a policy, in private reality, which is the precise opposite of public profession, has ever been a characteristic of certain elements of the "Left," Notable in this respect has been the denial of free speech to opponents.

For years Conservative meetings were broken up by organised Red violence. This "Left", which stood so pre-eminently and vociferously for freedom of speech under "Democracy", and later fought a world war in its name, had for years past denied that freedom at home to all who held contrary opinions. That did not matter much to Conservatism, in all large industrial areas they brought, at any rate, their larger meetings to an end, in favour of the pure formality of ticketed meetings of their supporters.

Red violence mattered not to them for they had the vast power of the Press through which to address and convert the Public. We had no such Press or resources. At that time the public meeting, and the platform appeal, were our only means of reaching the ear of the people. We had to preserve that freedom or perish.

The "Left" came to break up our meetings, as they had done those of Conservatives—after due warning they went out; great was the howl of indignation! By preserving the right to speak at our own meetings we were "denying free speech"; by preserving order, and protecting our audiences from violence at our own meetings, we were "creating disorder." In paradox so grotesque that it cannot be acceptable even to the traditional "infantilism of the Left," (as Lenin described it), but only to the petulant imbecilism which its degeneracy has produced, we were finally accused of creating disorder at our own meetings, with the only possible effect of denying ourselves, free speech! So, when the corpse is found with a knife in the back, the only possible explanation is that "it did it itself."

However, these problems were in time overcome, entirely by our own exertions. Many of our members were seriously injured at their own meetings; my own sojourn in hospital was confined to a week. Whether we had so injured ourselves at our own meetings for the purposes of advertisement, or masochistic satisfaction, was never very clearly explained by our opponents. They, at any rate, hastened to pass legislation to hamper us, as far as possible, in the work of protecting ourselves, and ensuring that audiences, who had come to our meetings to hear a speech, would not be prevented from hearing it by organised violence.

The Old Parties, however, who thus long before the war, formed a coalition in Parliament against us, did not on any occasion go so far as to enact that if an Englishman, or his wife, were slashed or threatened by a razor, he must not respond with a blow of his fist. Consequently, order was secured, and preserved at our meetings, for years before the war, and record audiences were able to hear the speech they had come to hear in peace and order.

We may be assured that all these attacks on meetings were the work of unauthorised hooliganism, and had nothing to do with the respectable elements of the Labour Party. These attacks were, of course, not promoted in any way by the Labour Leadership, but, it must be noted that, within my knowledge at any rate, no responsible Labour leader at that time condemned them, or appealed for order at our meetings. Their only contribution to free speech, in this phase, was to prohibit the use of loud speakers in the London Parks, which they then controlled; directly our meetings began to exceed the size which can be addressed by the human voice and, still worse, to surpass in magnitude the Labour meetings at which they had used these instruments for years. On the other hand, when our vital elements in East London, which contrasted strikingly with the dull ineptitude of the local Labour Parties, had swung, at any rate, the youth of that area almost solidly to our side[1], and an uncontrollable exuberance led to the break-up of Labour Leaders' meetings, public appeals were addressed to me by some of that Leadership to restore order at their meetings! They omitted to note that their Party had combined beforehand with the Conservative Party to pass a .strangely-named Public Order Act, whose avowed object, inter alia, was the prevention of discipline and control over our members, which was maintained by the practical method of a distinctive dress that rendered them easily recognisable. Meantime, loud swelled the clamour from Labour platform and Press against "Fascist Thugs"; how quickly and easily they forgot that the meetings of their opponents, whether Conservative or Fascist, had been smashed for years, before ever a word of opposition was spoken at their own meetings.

---

1   In the Municipal Elections of 1937, British Union polled 23 per cent of the votes recorded in one area in East London, and over 19 per cent of the votes recorded in all seats contested in that area. This was, of course, an old people's vote, as few of the young have votes in Municipal Elections, and it was the young who formed our Movement in East London. In general, while the break-up of meetings served their purpose, the "Left" was silent; When that instrument turned against them they whined: When their opponents were finally silenced, by other means, they used it as an argument for keeping them in gaol: But these are studies for the pathologist rather than the psychologist; and these relatively trivial matters, which belong to the long past, are only mentioned here for one reason. They serve to illustrate and emphasise one of the main themes of the present work, that it has ever been the consistent and persistent purpose of the "Left" (that warrior champion of free speech at the expense of other people's lives) to deny free speech at home to all opponents and, in particular, to those whom they most feared. Conservatism, to its dishonour, was prepared to join to some extent in the racket for suppressing people it considered dangerous to its interests, even by means which had been used against itself, once it was assured that its Press Power rendered it immune from such methods.

The idea is what the Parties ever feared. Everything else has been merely the barrage of falsehood behind which they advanced to the suppression of the idea. To this end organised attacks were made upon our meetings, while the Press sought to fasten on us, first the charge of creating disorder at our own meetings and, secondly, the charge of brutality, because we dared to restore order by ejecting armed hooligans. To this end, also, not only the Press, but, the Money Power of the "Right" combined with the local power of the "Left" to deny us, for public meetings, many halls throughout the country which were mostly controlled by large interests of the "Right," or by local authorities dominated by the "Left." These methods, of course were only subsidiary to the main assault, when a coalition of all the Old Parties in Parliament rushed through special legislation, which was aimed expressly at crippling the progress of our Movement, and no other. Yet all failed to arrest an Idea, which, by its whole character, innate truth, historic necessity and vital force, was stronger than all material things.

Then, they had their war, and that gave all the little stay-at-home people of all varieties, their supreme opportunity. The idea could be suppressed, and its protagonists silenced in prison, by the whispered suggestion that they must be traitors to their country, because they thought that war unnecessary. We were at war and that was the excuse for everything. Any little man who had ever failed to answer our argument, and never dared to meet us in Public Debate, could stand with "security" the other side of the prison bars grimacing his defiance and jabbering his insults. Every little man, with a "hush-hush" job, could flatulate his innuendoes over the cocktails, which he could never afford, in such inspiring quantities, when his own abilities in business had to pay for them, instead of a salary provided by the taxpayer. What a chance for every mediocrity and dunce on the fringe of politics; for every little "Tadpole" and "Taper," to strut his little hour. Serious critics were all in gaol, and even the Communists were singing "Rule Britannia," because "Holy Russia" was on our side, and bleeding out a stolid resistance to the vast bulk of the German Armies. Fine was that evening and deep the heady draughts of "democratic" wine. What mattered the morrow? — when Stalin was so matey and the supplies were getting through to Archangel!

All, in this phase, was easy going for those elderly gentlemen who are ever ready to die vicariously for the right of others to express their opinions, as long as their own particular opponents can be put in gaol, whenever they become really inconvenient. To such purpose was evolved the ingenious technique of keeping the Habeus Corpus Act on the Statute Book, as a monument of British Liberty, but suspending its chief provisions in any testing period, when its operation could serve the very purpose for which it was originally designed. It was easy going during the war because any opponents of their policy could be represented as a menace to the "Security of the State," in the inevitable hysteria of the period.

Since the war was over, things have not been quite so easy for the "freedom lovers." The plea of keeping men in gaol for "security" reasons could scarcely be sustained when "security" was plainly beyond doubt, as a consequence of overwhelming victory. The plea that men should be kept in prison, because they wanted Peace and Friendship with Foreign Governments, could scarcely be maintained when those Governments had ceased to exist. The suggestion, as grotesque as it was insulting, that a "fifth column"[2] could menace this country, would hardly hold water when all other columns had plainly been destroyed.

So the great excuse, founded on the great lie of the "Left," came to an end, and the prison gates swung open with a reluctant clang.

---

2   This insult might at least have been retracted at an earlier date, when the Prime Minister, Mr. Churchill, observed on November 5th, 1940,' three years before my release: "Fifth Column activities—if there were any over here, and I am increasingly sceptical—would prove wholly ineffective." Although his Government kept us in gaol it does not appear that he thought he had a "fifth column" then! On the other hand, it seems that he is very certain he has got one now! For he said at Fulton, U.S.A. on March 5th, 1946: "However, in a great number of countries far from the Russian frontiers and throughout the world, Communist fifth columns are established and work in complete unity and absolute obedience to the directions they receive from the Communist centre." Such is Nemesis!

My Answer

Our opponents of the "Left" were then faced with a necessity which they have ever found painful—within the limited means at their disposal—the necessity of thinking again. The result of this process produced both its cruder and subtler manifestations. It was stated earlier in these observations that I was obliged for the new agitation to prevent me from publishing books, because it illustrated the point I had to prove. Such an agitation when the war is over, tears to shreds the suggestion that these people desired our imprisonment, and silence, for any other reason than the desire to suppress our opinions. It would prove for me my point—that this was the reason behind the agitation for our imprisonment—without me uttering another word; so far as this controversy goes I could merely write Q.E.D., across the latest effusions of my opponents. For this new agitation, after the war, is plainly directed to this end, and to no other; in fact, it can have no other purpose, and not even the most credulous could believe that it had. These opponents are now driven to abandoning all excuse and innuendo: they have come out, openly and brazenly, on the grounds that they dislike and fear our opinions—so they must be suppressed. Thus at last we are all agreed at least on one point; their consistent motive throughout is now revealed, beyond a shadow of a doubt. Therefore, I repeat, for the new agitation I am much obliged to them.

The new campaign takes two forms. The first is very simple; we must be debarred from expressing our opinions merely because we are ourselves. The Executive should be given the power, by Order, at least to prohibit any right of expression to anyone whom the majority in Parliament, at the time, regard as a danger to their ideas. What the difference is between this system and the ideas they allege they have been righting against, these warrior philosophers have not yet seen fit to explain. In the light of all recent protestations such an attitude is, of course, a little too crude for the subtler minds among our opponents. It is difficult for anyone with a sense of the ridiculous to assume this position, when he has assured the world for some years that he was fighting a world war to affirm Voltaire's principle— "I may detest what you say, but will die to defend your right to say it."

So they reject the idea of new laws, in favour of a good rummage through the dustbin of discarded statutes. And, let it be observed, almost anyone in the country could be locked up for the breach of some law which has never been repealed, but has fallen into desuetude. Reference is made here to laws of the past and long past, not merely to the host of incomprehensible war-time regulations, by which the new bureaucracy still retains the power to imprison anyone it wishes, on some charge or other. On the subject of old statutes, I have even heard it suggested (without ever verifying it) that anyone can be imprisoned who does not go to Church every Sunday. At any rate, few modern thinkers and philosophers would remain long at large if, for instance, the Blasphemy Laws, still on the Statute Book, were literally applied. Certainly the many laws protecting the Royal Family could not only have placed in gaol their vicious assailants among the Communists in the present century, but, also, the serious leaders of Republican Movements, like Chamberlain and Dilke, during the last century, who afterwards rose to be pillars of the State without that classic but painful prelude to greatness! Somewhere a law exists to put anyone in gaol; it is a happy thought for some minds.

The situation of our opponents, however, was not so felicitous as may at first appear. For the stalwart protagonists of class war, with characteristic lack of all sense of humour, emerged triumphant, from profound researches, with lines culled from the book of old statutes, which indicated that it was an offence "to raise discontent or disaffection among His Majesty's subjects, or to promote feelings of ill-will or hostility among different classes of such subjects." Perhaps, when we call these industrious students "protagonists of class war," we may have to qualify this description by adding that they merely supported the Party when it had become safe and respectable, after its foundation had been securely laid in "class war" by its pioneers! The idea, as usual, came to the above-mentioned "stalwarts" from elsewhere, as it so happened that some gentleman of whom I know nothing, and who may have nothing whatever to do with the Labour'

Party, or any interest in the matter beyond a disinterested study of the laws of his country, wrote to our leading "intellectual" weekly suggesting this form of words. His idea was soon widely canvassed in "Pink" circles, and taken up with avidity by the above mentioned stalwarts of the class war. The correspondent, in pursuit of his academic point, had offered to subscribe a few guineas for a prosecution under these words and as he used the term "Fascist" we can only presume that he possibly meant us! I wrote promptly to this journal offering to add a few poor guineas of my own to the good cause, as no-one, had been more frequently assailed on grounds of class! The journal in question is ever ostensibly a paragon of fair-minded impartiality, in matters of free speech, but their intellectual probity was strained, apparently a little too far at the idea of permitting a brief reply to a Fascist, and the letter did not appear. So great was the glee of the enemy, unhampered by any necessity for dealing with any retort; a very fair and "democratic" position.

But the words in question rippled far beyond the narrow "intellectual" circle of their origin. The old heroes of class war woke again; the speeches of the late Mr. Bob Williams (then a member of the Labour Party Executive, and later elected Chairman of that Party) rang again in their ears; and they remembered the cheers of the faithful, when he threatened to "run up the Red Flag on Buckingham Palace." The great slogans of the past thrilled again in their hearts, the fervent denunciations of "capitalist wars"; the roaring shouts against the "bloodsucking class" of "capitalists, "who exploited the workers"; "down with the landlords"; down with the "classes" (whatever they were); down with everybody and everything, so long as the Labour Party could climb up! Someone had inadvertently provided the Labour Party with an idea and great was the enthusiasm (as it was a silly one). So forth rushed the warriors of class war to tell the world that, if Mosley dared move, he would be prosecuted under existing law for promoting "hostility between classes."

A normal interpretation of the words in question would appear applicable to their own performances in the past and, on occasion, to their antics in the present, but not to what they had in mind for the future; because they had ever defined "Capitalists" as a class (ever since Old Whiskers wrote "*Das Kapital*"; which became a bible to the few of them who could understand it, and a "Totem" to the rest); but no-one, to my knowledge, has ever defined the Jews as a class.

For my part, anything which I ever have to say about the Jewish problem will be a sober and serious discussion of a matter which is universally discussed. No law has yet been enacted to secure that anything may be discussed from the Crown to Religion except the Jewish problem. If ever such a law is passed the British Public will draw their own conclusions.

As for the past, I ask my readers to judge from chapter six of "*Tomorrow We Live*" reprinted in this volume to enable them to give their judgment on the question, whether or not it was true to suggest that I, or my friends, stood for "torture and murder" of Jews, or for "racial persecution." They will see from this official policy of our Movement, published in 1938, that such a suggestion was not merely a travesty of what we said, but a complete contradiction of it. To suggest that the Jews should have a National Home where they could become a Nation was, in our view, the way to end racial hostility, and even persecution, which was liable to arise from the situation then existing. Even exchanges in the heat of controversy, when we had been bitterly attacked by various Jewish elements, never suggested anything of that kind.

I speak here, of course, in this whole matter in respect of the policy of British Union—not for that "lunatic fringe" of Fascism, which found expression in various small independent societies of infinitesimal membership and inflated egotisms. Remote from the struggle and dust of the arena, they divided their time between abusing us who had carried our cause not through back drawing rooms, but through public meetings to a great national movement, and publishing crude absurdities about Jews, which could have no other effect than to swing the average Englishman to their side. The deficiency of these people arose from the head rather than from the character; they were honest but incredibly stupid; their only fault of character was a vanity out of all proportion to their capacities. Quite unwittingly, therefore, they served the cause which they most detested. No weapon in English politics is more effective than caricature, and no caricature is so effective as a living caricature. These people were walking caricatures of a Fascist Movement, and, of course, our opponents took every opportunity to parade their "idiosyncrasies." If they had paid the greatest living caricaturist ten thousand a year to caricature a Fascist Movement on paper, they could not have served this purpose so effectively as by merely reproducing, on appropriate occasion, something which these curious creatures had said or done.

No references to the Jewish problem, other than those previously published at the beginning of 1938 in *Tomorrow We Live* will appear in this volume, as I desire that our story in this matter should be considered objectively, and with the minimum of passion, in order that fair-minded readers should decide for themselves, whether it was fair to suggest that our policy in this respect meant "murder." Then, if they are further interested in the subject of murder, let them study the attitude of those who led the mobs which howled for my assassination in prison. Further studies in murder may be suggested by later reflections of the present essay.

But the reader, who studies our policy, in this or in other matters, may be moved by a favourite line of attack upon us to say "Oh, yes, that is all right, but it is only a policy to get power, and afterwards they would have done the opposite." Perhaps "guilt" sensations again invade the psychological background of the "Democrat" who makes the charge. He is sub-conscious of the election pledges given in Britain during the election of 1935, and during the last Presidential Election in America, before that country entered the war. Let anyone who is interested in the technique of obtaining power, by promising exactly the opposite of what is afterwards done, study the pledges of those two occasions, in the light of what subsequently occurred. In making this charge, the so-called "democrat" is once again merely judging others by himself, and accusing them of intending to do what his own leadership has done already. In the absence of the test of fact, we can only ask people to judge us by our character and record. If any man thinks I have gone through so much in order, at the end, to do the opposite of anything I have ever said, and to betray everything for which I have ever stood, I can only reply that he will never understand me, and I shall never understand him; our paths, therefore, lie in different directions.

But let us return briefly, before considering the results of the policy which we opposed, to the unfortunate dilemma of our opponents, which arose when they could no longer keep us in gaol for "security" reasons. We found the more intelligent searching legal dustbins for obsolete laws whose application, only a generation ago, would have placed some leaders of their own Movement in gaol; while the less intelligent demanded what amounts to "retrospective" tests, with a view to removing the right to publish our opinions.

This latter point is worth examining further before we leave the subject, as we have already seen something of it, and it still echoes in the world. This new "burning of the books," or more effective modern version of the process by suppressing them before they are published is, of course, to apply only to "'Fascists"; that is, to anyone whose opinions they fear will, fundamentally and effectively, challenge their own. A fine liberality of 'free speech" is, naturally, still to be accorded to those who do not differ with them about anything that really matters! What is their definition of a "Fascist"?; it is, of course, anyone who at a certain date belonged to a certain organisation. Although, at the date in question, this organisation was perfectly legal and no-one ever questioned, or can now question, the legal right to belong to it, our new witch hunters now suggest that such membership should incur certain penalties in the future.

My Answer

The penalty is, in one way or another; (preferably by the direct selection of new law and, if not, by indirect pressure) to prevent a person who has been a member in the past of a perfectly legal organisation, from expressing his opinions in the future. Let us reduce the proposition to its logical absurdity. In July 1939, it was perfectly legal and indeed commonplace to walk clown Piccadilly wearing a moustache. But anyone who took advantage of the freedom so universally accepted at the time, and, indeed, then widely advertised to the world at large, must now incur certain penalty. If, in fact, he walked down Piccadilly in 1939 wearing a moustache, he must, in 1946, refrain from walking out at all. At any rate, to mark the popular displeasure he might be debarred from walking out with his trousers on!

Such are the clowning absurdities which can be reached, once we push, to its logical conclusion, the principle of retrospective disability for something which at the time was perfectly legal and proper. Who knows today, in perpetrating the most innocent action, that he will not incur penalty or disability tomorrow, if such retrospective principles are enshrined in Law? It is for this reason that British Law, and all other law founded on that massive basis whose values have survived the stern tests of two thousand years of European civilisation, have rejected any suggestion of the retrospective principle. And, to be fair to them, all major parties of the State in recent times have rejected in Parliament all suggestions of introducing the retrospective principle into the Law of Great Britain. While Law survives that principle cannot enter, for its entry replaces Law by the unfettered whim of arbitrary power. When Law is set aside it enters inevitably; for instance, when Habeus Corpus was effectively suspended in favour of 18B, such considerations at once arose—Before the war you knew so and so, and stood for such and such—We will keep you in gaol for it. It was useless to reply that Mr. Chamberlain had seen them since I had, and that he was not locked in gaol for it! Arbitrary will, in retrospective survey, had replaced law; the same action could be right in one person and wrong in another.

Take my own case, further, as an illustration of what might happen to anyone under such a dispensation (well, anyone, perhaps it should be added, of lively temperament and energetic habits). I had met the German leader twice in my life, in April 1935 and October, 1936. On both occasions he invited me to lunch and we discussed at some length the interests of Britain and Germany, with the result that we came to the conclusion that no inherent reason existed for friction or conflict between them. It is not too much to say that these two lunches and two conversations contributed substantially to my three and a half years sojourn in gaol. The Italian leader I had also not met since 1936, but, although he never invited me to lunch, knowing him, too, was much held against me. Your fault, my critics will reply, for not foreseeing that three years later we should be at war with these two Powers, and the Old Gang would get you under 18B. I must plead guilty to not possessing second sight, but also affirm that, as someone who got about a bit, I seemed bound to be caught one way or the other by this principle if I was unpopular enough with the ruling parties to make my imprisonment desirable in their eyes.

In the last few years before the war I was pinned at home by the immense and continuous labours which the great growth of our Movement imposed on me. In my earlier days, and particularly before the birth of the Fascist Movement, I had seized every opportunity to travel, not only because it interested me, but, also because it appeared desirable that anyone in active politics should know as many as possible of the Foreign Statesmen with whom he might one day be called upon to deal. Personal contacts and friendships have broken in our time and sight the barriers of many difficulties; therefore, when time allowed, throughout my life I have travelled much. So the reader must sympathise with the hopelessness of my position, or of anyone like me, in any situation of war, if Habeus Corpus were always suspended and a retrospective 18B probe applied in the absence of Law, on the simple and now familiar lines—You knew so and so, we are at war with his country, and we think you are a menace anyhow; so off to gaol you go! This principle would nearly always have caught me whoever we were fighting, except perhaps, in the case of war with Russia, where my notorious dispute with the Communists would, presumably, save me.

If, for instance, we had been fighting America in 1939, instead of Germany,my situation might have been even worse. For some years before, I had not merely lunched with Mr. Roosevelt, but had accompanied him on a protracted fishing trip in his boat down the Florida Keys. My long retrospective offence would no doubt have been enhanced by the fact that I had always considered the idea of a conflict between Britain and America to be a fantastic crime. Ah!, but you were a National Socialist or Fascist, and the countries with which we were at war were also National Socialist or Fascist—retorts the bright-eyed critic — that was different. To him I reply that, after so much comment upon it, he might do us the honour of reading our policy even eight years after it was published; a little information sometimes restricts eloquence, but a grasp of the facts is also a fair substitute for a loose tongue. How much bearing that last, and frequent, observation had either on the situation or on our patriotism, the critic, and also the impartial reader, can study for themselves in the Foreword to *Tomorrow We Live*, reprinted in this volume after a first publication in 1938.

These simple reductions to absurdity of "Democratic" war-time practices, merely illustrate the difficulty and the danger which arises when Law is set aside in favour of some retrospective principle. It is not so funny when you do three and a half years in the gaols or concentration camps of "Democracy" because, in a moment of passion and hysteria, such a principle had temporarily replaced British Law. So we should note carefully when even a small movement within a large Party, seeks to introduce such a provision into the normal and permanent structure of our Law. All should note it carefully because, once established, that principle can be used to destroy anyone.

But it is not enough for an Englishman merely to look at home, now that the Law of Britain has again replaced the arbitrary creation of retrospective offence. Let him look, also, abroad, in the consciousness of his obligations before History, during a period which, he is frequently assured, reposes in his hand supreme power and influence. The ordinary man may not know the intricacies of International Law, which is a matter for those learned in the Law. I do not myself profess to understand them. But he can instruct his statesmen and representatives to ensure that, in no circumstances, shall the first principles of Law be violated by the creation of retrospective offences. What was legal at the time a thing was done remains legal; it only becomes illegal in the future if new law is created, and proclaimed, so that all may be aware of it. Then a man, who violates existing law, is rightly subject to whatever penalties are laid down. But if a man is punished for something which was legal at the time he did it, the crime is committed not by him but by the Parties who create retrospective offences and penalties. If a man is killed because he did something which, under established and existing law, was legal, this act, by every law which in our consciousness is known to God, and by every law so far known to man in the long and majestic traditions of British and European Law, is murder, and bears no other name.

For my part, I repeat, I do not profess to know or to understand International Law, and no-one, not learned in the Law, can make such profession. I do not possess the expert knowledge necessary to determine, with certainty and proof, whether things done in Europe during these times are in accord with International Law, or whether that Law, and the basis of all Laws, has been violated by various Governments in the political creation of retrospective offences. We only know that historians versed in these matters will search the records of these times for centuries. If, in fact, men are found to have been killed for doing what was legal at the time they did it, the verdict of History will be murder. I would save my country, if it were possible, from any chance of such stigma and, therefore, I ask my fellow countrymen, even in moments of savage passion, to instruct their representatives to ensure that, not only at home, but also abroad, where British influence and honour counts for anything, the retrospective offence shall not be created by political action in violation of Law. The application of existing Law is not our business but that of a Court, whose actions we cannot criticise, and which merely carries out the laws laid down by Governments and Parties; but the creation of new Law is our business, and every citizen has the right and the duty to discuss it.

To return now to the origin of this essay, the reader was asked at the beginning to judge for himself, from the works published in this volume, whether during the recent war we could rightly be put into prison or into concentration camps, because we held these opinions. That judgment I leave with confidence to all fair-minded readers of this volume. But another question was posed at the beginning of this essay —"whether, in the light of subsequent events, those opinions were proved right or wrong?" In dealing with this matter I must not be led into a study of the present and the future, because that is the subject of another book, which I hope will be ready soon after the present volume. The present book is intended entirely as a retrospect; it deals with the past alone and should not touch the present and the future.

So, in answering here, the question whether this policy was "proved right or wrong," I will not speak myself, but will give place to words spoken while I write by the main architect of the policy I opposed. In fact, when I read those words I was tempted to set aside this essay and to publish instead extracts from Mr. Churchill's speech at Fulton, Missouri, with the sole observation—"that is my case." I had to "give silence for Mr. Churchill" during the war, and I willingly "give silence" for him now; when he reviews the results of the policy which I was gaoled for opposing:-

"Nobody knows what Soviet Russia and its Communist International Organisation intends to do in the immediate future, or what are the limits, if any, to their expansive and proselytizing tendencies."

The reader of any of the works in this volume, whether published before or during the last war, will have observed our constant argument that to fight Germany, where no British interest was involved, would be to create a Russia-Communist danger to threaten every British interest. The reader will further have noted the recurrent theme that to join with Russia against Germany in the name of liberty, on an issue such as the return to her of the German city of Danzig, where that factor was actually inverted, would be finally to place European liberty at the mercy of Russia. But further silence for Mr. Churchill:

"From Stettin, in the Baltic, to Trieste, in the Adriatic, an iron curtain has descended across the Continent." (The creation of an "iron curtain" across the Continent appears a rather more serious matter than the abolition of a "corridor" across East Prussia).

"Behind that line lie all the capitals of the ancient States of Central and Eastern Europe — Warsaw, Berlin, Prague, Vienna, Budapest, Belgrade, Bucharest, and Sofia. All these famous cities and the populations around them lie in the Soviet sphere, and all are subject in one form or another, not only to Soviet influence, but to a high and increasing measure of control from Moscow."

Again, such "increasing measure of control" over entirely foreign peoples, who were relatively independent before we fought for "liberty," would appear to be a rather more serious matter than pre-war German efforts to get "control" of purely German populations; to say nothing of the extent of the present area of conquest and subjection, which is far greater than anything even in question before we gave Poland her guarantee (what reading that guarantee makes now!) But let Mr. Churchill further describe the manner in which our war aims have been realised:

"The Communist Parties, which were very small in all these Eastern States of Europe, have been raised to pre-eminence and power far beyond their numbers, and are seeking everywhere to obtain totalitarian control." ("Comrades," not "Quislings," now!) "Police Governments are prevailing in nearly every case, and so far, except in Czechoslovakia, there is no true democracy." (Call it 18B and make it respectable, if you don't want to offend Comrade Stalin!). "Turkey and Persia are both profoundly alarmed and disturbed at the claims that are made upon them, and at the pressure being exerted by the Moscow Government."

Really my task is done; controversy is made too easy when our opponents thus describe their own handiwork. Long ago I went out of business as a satirist when confronted by the Labour Government of 1931; feeling that man cannot gild the lily; you cannot make more ridiculous what nature has created in the image of perfect absurdity. Now, in the present situation, not of Comedy but Tragedy, I feel impelled to cease even the role of pedestrian political commentator, when our darkest prophecies of 1939 are painted in even more sombre lines by the master hand whose political triumph created the scene which he now depicts. In fact, every instinct of self-preservation should now impose upon me a voluntary silence; for, if this goes much further, the English will never forgive me for having been so right! Nevertheless, we must follow Fate through to the end, so let Mr. Churchill conclude:

"Whatever conclusions may be drawn from these facts— and facts they are " (Yes, facts at last), "This is certainly not the liberated Europe we fought to build up. Nor is it one which contains the essentials of permanent peace."

Once again, I know that I should merely write Q.E.D. across the page of ingenuous confession, but who could resist, on such an occasion, a quotation from Mr. Eden, who blinked his bewilderment in the House of Commons on Thursday, March 14th, 1946, with the observation:

> "We would all of us have hoped that this debate could have taken place in a smoother international setting. Six or nine months ago I could never have thought that that setting could be such as it is tonight."

Yet readers of this book will observe that it was possible to foresee that situation not merely six or nine months ago, but six or nine years ago. For this not one jot of credit is claimed by the author of this volume. Any child should have been able to foresee it; provided, of course, that he had the opportunity to devote his time to the study of politics and was not engaged, like the mass of the people, in other occupations which left them only sufficient leisure to be deceived by Press and Politicians.

Be that as it may, Mr. Churchill now faces the facts, and, as he puts it, "facts they are." Either friend or opponent must recognise him as a man of genius; to deny that quality in a man, merely because he is an opponent, is to admit the possession of a small, mean character, animated chiefly by a gnawing inferiority complex; e.g., those Socialists who ran to him to save them when they were frightened out of their silly wits, and covered him with abuse so soon as the danger was past.

Genius will not permit a man to ignore the main tendencies of his age, whether the policy he devises to meet them is entirely mistaken or, by some strange accident, right.

What of the vastly inferior character and intellect of the Socialist Leadership, with which "Democracy" hastened at the last election to replace a degree of will and talent that, within such a system, can only temporarily be tolerated, during the crisis and disaster of its own creation. The Socialist Leadership, of course, refuses to face the facts. They are, in fact, to be found in a very characteristic position; their muffled voices are heard dimly from the very deep sands, where their heads repose, repeating one of those monotonous chants of magic incantation which ever occur to them and other primitive organisms in moments of danger: "Uno, Uno, Uno, Uno." We can only reply that "we do know"; in fact, we have had some before—lots of it—packets of it. We even remember the League of Nations! So, as usual in the affairs of the present system, broad farce masks tragedy until once again supreme crisis tears through the mummery.

It has been my fixed purpose to write these words without passion. How great a strain that imposes may be conceived by those who regard with our eyes the picture presented by our country, and by that Europe which shares with us the sublime heritage of culture whose resplendent rays shone forth from Early Hellas, not only to illuminate the centuries of European History, but to tinge with glory all that is fine and noble in the thought of the American Continent. Let my passion not intrude, but let Mr. Churchill speak again on the results of this war:

> "When I stand here this quiet afternoon I shudder to visualise what is actually happening to millions now and what is going to happen in this period when famine stalks the earth. None can compute what has been called "the unestimated sum of human pain.""

For my part I feel, in all that humility which a sense of vast tragedy imposes, some pride in having striven to avert that dreadful "sum of human pain." Let us again follow the gaze of Mr. Churchill to the centre of that agony: where the tragic succession of the system operates once more, and ineptitude follows malice to complete by mass starvation the ruin which the bomb began.

> "The Russian dominated Polish Government has been encouraged to make enormous and wrongful inroads upon Germany, and mass expulsions of millions of Germans on a scale grievous and undreamed of are now taking place."

Undreamed of, no doubt, in the days when a few frontier adjustments in Eastern Europe and relatively trivial transfers of population in the orderly fashion of peaceful times, might have satisfied German requirements for living space, if one-tenth of the energy and goodwill had been devoted to finding a solution of her problem in 1939, or long before, that is now being given to "appeasing" the Soviet. If it be replied that she would never have been satisfied, I make the simple answer, why, at any rate, could it not be tried? Few will deny that it would have been more sensible to strive to the last for Peace, while arming to the utmost against the possibility of war, than to discard both armaments and efforts for Peace; which was the pre-war policy of the "Left" and much of the "Right."

Then it was a question, at most, whether Germany should be permitted to bring leadership and order to regions in which no British interest was involved, but from which backward and anarchic populations had constantly threatened European Peace. The suggestion, so shocking to some characters, was made, that a higher civilisation should guide a lower. (Here I am aware of greatly offending much current opinion by suggesting that a higher and a lower can exist in cultural achievement, or even in nature. To follow that opinion to its logical end we have to affirm that Isaac Newton was in no way a higher type than a circus clown, or even than the inmate of a lunatic asylum. This "complex," for it cannot be described as a process of thought, originates from a system which often gives privilege to the unworthy, instead of affording position and honour only to those whose abilities merit that opportunity and distinction, and whose energies deserve it).

However, now that the position in Eastern Europe is reversed, and it is rather a question of the domination of the higher by the lower, a different view is naturally taken by certain psychological types whose deepest instincts are thereby satisfied. To subject the Teuton to the Slav gives to such people a sense of deep, spiritual satisfaction, relieving many well-founded complexes of inferiority in their own psychologies. Take the land which is elevated by a long line of illustrious names in literature, philosophy, science, music and poetry, who, with the understanding of kinship, reach through the glory of our own Elizabethan age to the original Hellenic inspiration of the European tradition roll that land in the mud, let the Moujik dance on their culture while you shout that they never had any; that process affords a deep contentment of the soul to types whose psychology permits of easy analysis. But to anyone with no feeling of inferiority, who is conscious not only of our Shakespeare and our Poetry, but of the whole great range of British Philosophy, Literature, and Science, whose names require no recitation to the educated Englishman, that spectacle must bring disgust, or the deeper emotion which I feel. Here and now I affirm simply this: the land and the people who share with us not only blood, but also the cultural heritage of Europe—the fairest gift mankind has known—cannot lie there. If that were the future Europe would lose her soul; and that shall not be.

But let us return to that limited sphere, which, in myopic vision, is wrongly regarded as the whole range of politics. We can now easily observe how simple has been the trick through which European civilisation has been wrecked. Pre-war reference will be found, later in this volume, to the virtual alliance which subsisted between the Soviet and the Democracies before the war, dating from the time of the Franco-Soviet Pact. Readers will remember the abrupt termination of that arrangement in favour of the transient Russo-German understanding, which carved up Poland while we stood as impotent spectators. Who can doubt that Russia's change of sides did much to precipitate the clash between the Democracies and Germany by encouraging the latter to think that her Eastern expansion, in agreement with the Soviet, would be a relatively easy matter which, at worst, would involve a one-front war, without any serious power of the West to interfere in her Eastern plans. Russia's temporary arrangement with Germany set the match to the whole powder magazine.

Yet to some extent the Soviet miscalculated; they probably reckoned that the great antagonists in the West would bleed each other to death on the lines of the 1914-18 war, and that their consequent exhaustion would leave Europe as easy prey to the Soviet "expansive and proselytizing tendencies" which Mr. Churchill now again discerns. It did not work out like that at the time, because Germany won too easily in the West for the concepts of the Soviet to fructify in the summer of 1940. Temporarily, at any rate, Germany could turn to the East with her back free in the West. In the final clash Russia was only saved by Anglo-American Intervention on the Continent, coupled with a steady stream of supplies, which she could not produce for herself, and the ceaseless activity of the Money Power in building up fresh Continental coalitions on traditional lines.

By what right of power, or of superior culture, then does Russia aspire to dominate a large area of the Continent; not merely to lead it by example or achievement? Let us imagine the position in the recent war reversed, with only 90 million Russians, in the middle of Europe, facing 170 million Germans on one side of her and the combined powers of Britain and America on the other. Would the struggle have lasted a month? That is the brief answer to Russian pretensions in terms of power. As for any claim to cultural leadership, I invite anyone who has reached, let alone surpassed the elementary school stage, to place the Literary, Philosophic and Scientific production of the Slav beside that of the Englishman or the German, not to mention the combined achievement of European civilisation in the last 2,600 years. (Hush-hush! I know that the King of the Cannibal Islands is just as good as Locke or Kant, and far superior to any classic Greek, because he is so much more "modern," and that a backward child can give instruction to any schoolmaster). Yet the fact remains that, largely by the exertions of the great Democracies, Russia has been given a position of Partial European hegemony, which may extend to completion, unless Britain and America are prepared to stay for longer than they wish in armed might on the Continent.

My Answer

Such is the result of the policy we opposed; and the success of that policy could never have produced any other result. Its full effect is, for the time being, mitigated by no virtue or achievement of the politicians. It so happens that Anglo-American scientists were the first to develop the "Atom Bomb." That is an event which cannot be ascribed wholly to chance, because it is more probable that our civilisation would lead in scientific matters than the Soviet-Slavonic system. But the contingency of the emergence of that weapon at this moment in our hands was not something which could be foreseen by politicians when they began this business. So far as they are concerned they were saved by luck, and nothing else, from far worse things. It was their particular fortune to have as their assistants scientists of genius at a decisive moment, when the cool, clear ray of the scientific future for the first time illuminated, with calm and blessed finality, the tortured human scene.

If they had to meet the Soviet system merely with man-power for man-power on the Continent, at the present time, what would have been the outcome in the present mood of the Democracies? Would their superior power have operated, or would "we want to go home" have prevailed? Or what would have happened, as Mr. Churchill again put it, "had the position been reversed" and some Communists had produced the Atom Bomb? Happily scientists, of the first order, are naturally loyal in entirety to their own countries, which by equal law of nature are numbered among the higher nations. Further, men with such genius for creation are, in any case, likely to hope for some higher emanation of the European mind and spirit than those first, relatively crude, reactions to the breakdown of an obsolete system, which are called Communism. The word of Spartacus was never yet the last; still less in an age when brain at length replaces brawn, and mind begins to prevail over mass and matter.

There we may leave the European scene, for purpose of this retrospect, with the observation that we do not owe even this uneasy equilibrium to the foresight or will of our politicians. Let us just remember that it all began when Germany wanted back in her territory the admittedly German city of Danzig. How rapidly such acorns grow into oaks if manured with sufficient stupidity and malice!

As already suggested, the purpose of this volume is not to provide a policy for the present or future, but to justify our position in the past. In relation to the present and the future some of the writings here reprinted are, of course, out of date, although a surprising amount of *Tomorrow We Live* written eight years ago, remains very relevant. But, on the whole, the intervening years have brought vast developments which no dynamic mind can ignore. It is my hope that readers of my next book will agree that my thought has developed in pace with events; it is my ambition to go some way beyond them. Any man whose thought has not developed in recent years has plainly ceased to think.

It has been justly remarked that science has crowded into the last five years as much development as usually takes place in fifty. This, surely, provides one of the most tragic reflections of our time, and poses a most pressing question; why do such great bounds in human thought and action only occur under pressure of war? Why are such bright blossomings of the mind and spirit only evolved in the bitter blast? Why is destruction rather than construction the dominant stimulus? It is not enough to reply that they will only pay for science when they are scared by war into taking an interest in it; e.g., they refused my request for a million pounds a year for medical science in the Labour Government of 1929, but later thought nothing of spending five hundred times as much on the Atom Bomb. To find the complete answer we must dig deep, not only beneath the structure of present society, but into the depths of that curious twisted psychology which this Society has produced. If we go deeper still into Nature—Phusis— herself, and the minds of her greatest students, we may find an answer yet more inimical to current thought. Not until we have found the answer to these, and many other, questions can the creative action of the future be rightly directed.

My Answer

All such, matters must await another book, which by its whole character must go far beyond anything more than suggested in this book. Some slight advantage has accrued to me in recent years in that I have been afforded ample opportunity for reading and reflection! As a result, the view occurred to me that it would be a good thing if men of action always retired for a considerable period in the middle of their lives for purposes of study and pure thought. At 49 I feel some benefit from that experience. It is curious and encouraging that the efforts of our opponents to destroy us sometimes have the reverse effect to that intended, at any rate, in the sphere of the mind and the spirit. This book, therefore, is certainly not my contribution to the present or to the future, and purports only to be a retrospect of the past.

In certain respect, however, the reader must be warned against too hastily regarding some sections of the writings here reprinted as obsolete, particularly in the region of economics. Let us take two examples, in which a superficial view might quickly dismiss certain passages as without relevance to the present. For instance, throughout the economic section of *TOMORROW WE LIVE* I was dealing with the economics of surplus, and we are now confronted with the economics of shortage. Then the question was, how to find a market for which we could produce; now the question is, how to produce enough to live on any reasonable standard. The politicians had never, in practice, found an answer to the first question, which I suggested lay in the increased power of the people to consume what they produced, within a new system of the State designed to secure that increased power in an orderly, but not bureaucratic, economy. (The "order" of industrial self-government, within the broad delimitations laid down by the State, is the opposite of Bureaucracy; yet within the present system they cannot conceive "planning" without Bureaucracy).

Temporarily, however, the problem was solved in a manner all too typical of the present system. Six years of war turned a surplus into a shortage. Any fool can burn down a house if he does not want to furnish it, or has not the energy to paint the walls. That was their

46

solution, quite inadvertent, of course, like all their actions. But the same situation will inevitably recur, even after the ravages of war, when a yet further increase in productive power has got into its stride, and has functioned during a sufficient period. Then we shall again see the destruction of wealth because it cannot be "sold," and science restricted because it can "produce too much"; unless a modern system to meet scientific facts emerges from economic chaos.

Another point arises, for example, in the economic argument, which may cause superficial misunderstanding. Much attention was concentrated in my writings on the "mobility" of capital at that period, and the power thereby conferred upon it, not merely to dominate the economic system, but also politics and Governments. As a result of war that power appears to the casual observer largely to have disappeared. Certainly, in this respect, the legacy of war has afforded to the present Labour Government an advantage which was not available to their predecessors, and is in no way due to their own courage and energy in facing High Finance.

With what speed, however, did they hasten to discard the weapons which Fate had thrust so fortuitously into their inadequate hands! For they at once began to ask the British people to sign international agreements, which deprived British Government of that new power and freedom in financial matters that previous Governments had lacked. So, while their ability to dominate the scene had been largely removed from financiers within the country, by necessary wartime measures like exchange control, an almost complete power over our economy has now been accorded to financiers outside the country. This has arisen from the war exhaustion of our resources, coupled with the Labour Government's typical reaction to the situation, in relying on an American Loan and signing the Bretton Woods Agreement which, again, subordinates our Empire economy to Finance—this time external.

In short, as a result of the war and the inability of British Governments to organise self-help, within the Empire, power passed from the City of London to Wall Street, New York. Labour Chancellors no longer glance nervously toward the City of London, as they did during my time as a Minister of the Crown, when I was trying to get things done within the system.

They can now even afford to put up a show of being rude to the "City"! Labour Chancellors, however, must now look with respect amounting to a helpless sycophancy across the Atlantic, if their international economy is not to crash. The greater the difficulties, the more complete must become the "dependence" of any Movement with the policy, structure and character of the Labour Party. Such stern tests differentiate sharply between different characters; the dynamic, in testing times, strives still harder for a vital independence; the lethargic just fumbles for the supporting hand of a strong friend. (Lethargy must be the characteristic of any Government operating within the inhibitions of the system, and born of its psychology; although a variation in type can occur for a short time in war, because temporarily the system is set aside. For an earlier example of this, study Athens under Pericles. Yet inevitably, before long, the temporary virtues vanish and the permanent vices return. Meantime, striking reason for giving that helping hand came from the other side of the Atlantic, when an American Minister, giving evidence in favour of the loan, observed that rejection would "pull the Empire closer and closer together. The British would produce films, feeding stuffs and machine tools. A Buy British Campaign would not be necessary. There would be only British goods to buy". Our American friends need have no fear; now, even more than in the past, it is quite beyond a Government of the present system to develop from that quarter of the Globe, which is British Empire (containing every raw material which industry can require), a system capable of affording a decent life to the British people, without dependence on Foreign Finance. Their whole system, character and psychology, combined with the crushing legacy of difficulty which their war has left, give to them only the alternatives of dependence or disaster.

The third course of self-help in the vast undertaking of Empire development is not open to them; if they attempted it, within the inhibitions of their system and the psychology it has created, they would only make a hopeless mess of it; and they know it. Dependence on the stronger is ever the destiny of such types and so, after a few of the usual postures and dissident braggings, they will accept that inevitable position in the new hierarchy of Nations to which their past blunders and present character have reduced them. Those with some feeling for community of blood and culture will cleave to America; those with little natural feeling in anything will cleave to Russia. The latter will be fewer, at any rate, until things have gone further, as the second category are still a minority in this country.

So, when the struttings of the platform, and the bleats of "Left" journalists, have subsided again into the customary torpor, they will all go quietly to bed and repeat in their dreams, if not in their waking hours, "Thank God for Uncle Sam, and the Atom Bomb."

Great is the power of America in the present scene; but she too in the end will be confronted by the developments of the future with another version of the same situation—and with the same Alternative. On that day we shall not be divided in spirit from those original elements of American civilisation, to whom she owes her present greatness.

Meantime, sombre is the scene, and bitter will be the disillusionment of yet another returning generation, who were told, as we were in 1914, that a new world would be born of their sacrifice. Once again, that world of mirage fades into a morass, where politicians flounder in the inevitable results of a policy whose end was always plain to those with eyes or time to see. All questions will be canvassed but nothing done; and universal jabber will make confusion worse confounded. The union of war will give place to the divisions of peace. The shrill voice of a thousand little egos will again drown clear command,

and inhibit resultant action; the ignoble will again overwhelm the noble achievement, if only for destruction, will again yield to purposeless babel. The young will wonder why, as once we wondered; when we too were young, and brushing from our eyes the blood and dust to glimpse a fairer world.

This thing must take the course of history and destiny; it will not be long. The old must be worked out to the end before new life can begin; this is the law of that nature which rules the lives of men within the will of God. When next, together, we turn our eyes toward the future, we may discern—rising like Phoenix from these ashes—the undying soul of England and the European man.

Part 3

Quotations

Extracts from Mosley's speeches and from papers supporting British Union, which define British Union attitude during the war, and prove that, for several years before the war, he and his friends had pressed for National Rearmament.

Mosley's Message To All British Union Members On 1st September, 1939

"To our members my message is plain and clear. Our country is involved in war. Therefore I ask you to do nothing to injure our country, or to help any other Power. Our members should do what the law requires of them, and if they are members of any of the Forces or Services of the Crown, they should obey their orders, and, in particular, obey the rules of their Service..... We have said a hundred times that if the life of Britain were threatened we would fight again . . . ."

Article By Mosley In *"Action"*, 9th May, 1940

"According to the Press stories concerning the invasion of Britain are being circulated .... In such an event every member of British Union would be at the disposal of the Nation. Every one of us would resist the foreign invader with all that is in us. However rotten the existing Government, and however much we detested its policies, we would throw ourselves into the effort of a united nation until the foreigner was driven from our soil. In such a situation no doubt ever existed concerning the attitude of British Union' - The Author was arrested a fortnight later, on May 23rd, 1940.

My Answer

"*Action*", 14th March, 1940

British Union's attitude, before and since the war, has been:—

(1) We want peace and do our utmost to persuade the British people to declare their will for peace:
(2) We are determined by every means in our power to ensure that the life and safety of Britain shall be preserved by proper defences until that Peace can be made"

Air Defence Scandal

"Action disagrees with Mr. Churchill on nearly every subject under the sun, and particularly in recent years with his foreign policy. But we agree with his indictment of the gross neglect of British defences. British Union pressed rearmament upon the Government long before they began it, and long before even Mr. Churchill advocated it. British Union believes that Britain should be in a position to defend herself against the attack of any nation in the world"
"*Action*", 15th October, 1938.

So Early As 1933

"We are not prepared to leave Great Britain in the helpless position which we occupy today, in face of the overwhelming air strength of other countries. Either their air strength must come down, or our air strength must go up."
"*Blackshirt*", June 24th, 1933.

Mosley's Olympia Speech

"We will immediately mobilise every resource of the nation to give us an Air Force equal in strength to the strongest in Europe. We will modernize and mechanise our Army, and at the end of that process our Army will cost less, but will be the most modern and effective striking force in the world".
"*Blackshirt*", June 15th, 1934.

Mosley, Speaking At Brighton, 12th July 1934

"A Blackshirt Government would raise a national defence loan for three purposes:—

- To give Britain immediate air strength,
- To modernise and mechanise our Army.
- To put the Fleet in proper condition to defend our trade routes..."

"Blackshirt", July 5th, 1935.

See also same policy in Mosley's Book, "Fascism, 100 Questions Answered", published, March, 1936.

Mosley, writing in *"Action"*, 15th October, 1938

"Modern wars are won by airmen and mechanics not by masses of barrack square infantry".

Editorial, *"Action"*, May 31St, 1938

"The policy of British Union is to make peace with Germany, but not to accept a position in the air, or in any other sphere, inferior to her or any other country in the world".

Quotations From British Statesmen on the Subject of Opposing War

These extracts make nonsense of the suggestion that a man must be a traitor to his country, because he opposes a war.

Mr. Lloyd George, on politicians who oppose wars. Speaking at Oxford in 1900, he said: "Is every politician who opposes a war during its progress of necessity a traitor? If so, Chatham was a traitor, and Burke and Fox especially; and in later times Cobden and Bright and even Mr. Chamberlain (Joseph), all these were traitors"

Earl of Chatham in 1777, when opposing a war he thought unnecessary. History supports his view. It is a shameful truth, that not only the power and strength of this country are wasting away and expiring, but her well-earned glories, her true honour and substantial dignity, are sacrificed.

In a just and necessary war to maintain the rights or honour of my country, I would strip the shirt from my back to support it. But in such a war as this, unjust in its principle, impracticable in its means, and ruinous in its consequences, I would not contribute a single effort, nor a single shilling. I do not call for vengence on the heads of those who have been guilty: I only recommend to them to make their retreat, let them walk off; and let them make haste, or they may be assured that speedy and condign, punishment will overtake them"

He would have got something worse than 18B in our time!

Extract from a letter of Mr. Ramsay Macdonald to *Leicester Pioneer* 8th August, 1914, just before he opposed the war of 1914-18

"There is no doubt whatever but that, when all this is over and we turn back to it in cold blood and read it carefully so as to ascertain why England has practically declared war on Germany, we shall find that the only reason from beginning to end in it is that the Foreign Office is anti-German and that the Admiralty was anxious to seize any opportunity of using the Navy in battle practice"

The reader is asked to contrast the tone and attitude of this politician, who was afterwards elected Labour Leader and twice became Prime Minister of Britain, with any utterances of the author of this volume which the reader cares to select.

Opening Passage of *The British Peace* By Oswald Mosley Published October, 1939

"The British people want peace. Anyone with any sense wants peace. The only question is whether peace can be won on conditions that are satisfactory. Before they make Peace the British people require to know that they can face the future with honour, with security, and with the prospect of a fine life. It is the purpose of this pamphlet to show that such a peace can now be made at any time the British people decide. British Union asks our people to make peace on the terms for which we have always stood before and since the war. Those terms are not improvised and changed in the manner of the Political Parties to meet emergencies of their own creation. Our terms of settlement are based on our whole philosophy of politics and life. For such an idea we have fought for the seven years of British Union's existence ..."

"First I will give the reader the four points of the *British Peace*, summarised in the popular slogans, "Mind Britain's Business" and "Briton's Fight for Britain Only" :—

"Four Points"

(1) We have no interest in the East of Europe, which is no concern of the British Empire; therefore we should cease to intervene in any Eastern Europe quarrel.

(2) We are determined at all times to defend and to maintain British Empire, but we have no interest in "Mandated Territories" which do not belong to British Empire.

(3) Britain can and must be strong enough to defend herself from any attack by any nation in the world, but should never intervene in foreign quarrels which do not concern Britain or the Empire.

(4) We desire a permanent peace and understanding among the great nations of the West of Europe, leading to the final security of all-round disarmament.

"Few, at any rate, will deny that the announcement of such Peace terms by a British Government, created by the declared will of the British People, would bring immediate peace. It would bring peace for the simple and obvious reason that nothing would be left to fight about"

Earls Court Meeting, July 16th, 1939, reported to be the largest indoor meeting ever held in any country

The Exhibition Hall at Earls Court had never been used before for a political meeting until it was crowded for a Peace meeting at which Mosley was the sole speaker on July 16th, 1939. It is over three times the size of the Albert Hall, which was the largest hall previously used for political meetings in Britain. It is also much larger than the Madison Square Hall, New York, or the Deutschland Hall, Berlin.

Earls Court was taken for this meeting after four previous meetings at the Albert Hall, which showed that hall was quite inadequate for the crowds desiring to attend.

At the Earls Court Meeting on July 16th, 1939, a mass demonstration of quite extraordinary enthusiasm occurred in favour of Peace. Yet a few weeks later, a united Press enabled a coalition of the Old Parties to take the country into war. So much for the "Voice of the People" under Financial Democracy. But the reader is asked to await Mosley's next book: *The Alternative* for an answer....... born of these experiences....... to the problem how the will of millions to live a fairer life can win through in face of the Money Power.

The closing passage of Mosley's speech at Earls Court Exhibition Hall, Sunday, 16th July, 1939

A prophecy that was wrong because the author claimed that the British People would have the will and power to prevent war.

"I ask this audience tonight whether or not we are going to give everything we have within us, not only material resources but our moral and spiritual being, our very life and our very soul, in holy dedication to England that she shall not perish, but shall live in greatness. We are going, if the power lies within us—and it lies within us because within us is the spirit of the English—to say that our generation and our children shall not die like rats in Polish holes. They shall not die but they shall live to breathe the good English air, to love the fair English countryside, to see above them the English sky, to feel beneath their feet the English soil. This heritage of England, by our struggle and our sacrifice, again we shall give to our children. And with that sacred gift, we tell them that they come from that stock of men who went out from this small island in frail crafts across storm-tossed seas to take in their brave hands the greatest Empire that man has ever seen; in which tomorrow our people shall create the highest civilisation that man has ever known. Remember, we say to our children, those who have gone before you. Remember those who through the centuries have died that Britain might live in greatness, in beauty and in splendour. Remember too that, in the spiritual values that our creed brings back to earth, these mighty spirits march beside you and you must be worthy of their company.

So we take by the hand these our children, to whom our struggle shall give back our England; with them we dedicate ourselves again to the memory of those who have gone before, and to that radiant wonder of finer and nobler life that our victory shall bring to our country. To the dead heroes of Britain, in sacred union, we say: like you we give ourselves to England—across the ages that divide us— across the glories of Britain that unite us—we gaze into your eyes and we give to you this holy vow—we shall be true—today—tomorrow— and forever—England lives"

Part 4

Statement written in Prison by Oswald Mosley

Sent to the Prime Minister and Members of Parliament. The Statement is dated 8th October, 1943 and analyses suggestions made against British Union members, together with the Regulation under which they were imprisoned; before they were even aware that the new Regulation had been framed by the Government and passed by Parliament the evening prior to their arrest. No reply was received from the Government.

I write this statement because some 86 per cent, of the British subjects of British origin, arrested under the 18B Regulations, were members of British Union with my leadership (vide figures in *Hansard*, Vol 376, Cols. 858 and 860). For nearly two and a half years many of us have been held in gaols or camps, with the result that a number of people have been led to believe that we have done something disloyal to our country. In fact nothing of the kind has been alleged against us by the Government; because they have never suggested that we have done anything since the war except conduct a political campaign in favour of a negotiated Peace. Further, no one has contended that we have ever broken any law.

Prior to the war we were denounced as an ultra-patriot organisation. For 7 years before this war we maintained an unceasing campaign to obtain the proper armament of our country, in the air, on the sea and on land. We opposed this war, but we strove for a British Empire strong against any possible attack; we stood for peace but also for strength. If any one really suspects that we desire to bring about the defeat of our country, it may be replied that a 7 years campaign to secure re-armament against defeat is a strange beginning to that design.

My Answer

To anyone who says that it is disloyal to oppose a war the test reply may be made in the words of Mr. Lloyd-George when he was opposing the Boer War:-

"Is every politician who opposes a war during its progress of necessity a traitor? If so, Chatham was a traitor and Burke and Fox especially, and in later times Cobden and Bright."

We can also summon to our aid the whole experience of British History in our reply to the insinuation that we may be rendered disloyal to our country by adherence to our National Socialist and Fascist creed, which—in a "character, policy, form and method suited to this country alone"—we have long striven to persuade our fellow countrymen to adopt. The fact that they were fighting the catholic Power of Spain did not render British Catholics disloyal to their country in the age of Queen Elizabeth. The fact that the ideas of the French Revolution were, in many respects similar to their own ideas, did not make distinguished British Radicals disloyal to their country during the wars with Napoleon. Still less does our creed, whose first tenet is love of country, make us disloyal to our own country in the modern age. Those who allege such a change in the character of Englishmen, impute a decline to which denial has been given in a practical form by very many of our members who have served throughout the present war in the Forces, and have fought bravely. It should also be stated, that, within my knowledge, all of us in these gaols who were old enough to fight in the last war did in fact fight for our country in that war. For instance, beside me in this gaol is a man who won both the D.S.O. and M.C in the last war, but has served, with his wife, two and a half years in prisons and camps during this war, because he was a member of British Union.

The loyalty of our members to our country is the natural result both of our creed and of our policy since the conflict began. For instance, after the declaration of war I published the following message to members of British Union:- "Our country is involved in war. Therefore I ask you to do nothing to injure our country, or to help any other Power. Our members should do what the law requires of them, and if they are members of any of the Forces or Services of the Crown, they should obey their orders and, in every particular, obey the rules of their Services. Such a message was the natural expression of our policy: on the one hand we wanted Peace; on the other hand we wanted Peace with Britain undefeated."

It was never suggested to us in the spring of 1940 that we had no right to exercise full freedom of speech. The Press supporting us did not receive the warning for which provision is made in the present law. Instead, the Government requested Parliament to pass a new Regulation which was apparently specifically designed to enable members of our organisation to be imprisoned (vide Hansard, 21st July, 1942, Col. 1518).

On the following day, 23rd May 1940, we were thrown into gaol by virtue of this new Regulation of whose very existence we were unaware. We were not arrested under the original Regulation 18B (1), which provides, inter alia, for detention on account of alleged "acts prejudicial to the public safety." We were arrested under the ad hoc Regulation 18B (1a), which provides for the detention of anyone who was a member of an organisation whose leaders "have had association" with the leaders of countries with which this country is now at war. That I had had "associations," before the war, of a perfectly legal and proper character, I have certainly never denied. I held it to be my duty, by personal contact or any other proper means, to make whatever contribution I could to the maintenance and building of World Peace. Such "associations" before the war were perfectly legal; I reiterate and emphasise that it has never been suggested by the Government that we have done anything since the war except carry on a political propaganda. Is not two and a half years imprisonment for entirely legitimate proceedings at least sufficient for my supporters?

My Answer

For well over two years now our organisation has been harmed, and it has been made an offence in law to carry on our propaganda. Anyone continuing such propaganda can consequently be convicted in the courts and sentenced at the most to two years imprisonment. Our principle has always been to obey the law, as we have often stated. Under present law we can, in effect, be required to do whatever the Government of the day may desire. Over 80 per cent, of our members, who were originally arrested, have since been released, and have performed various forms of national service without complaint against them. Those still detained are just the same kind of people; why keep them rotting in prison and camps?

In any case it is very wrong that our fellow countrymen should be given occasion to think that we have done something disloyal to our country during this war; while in fact, during the private inquiry of the Government, nothing of the kind was suggested against us. No one can show that I or my friends have ever done anything disloyal to our country, and, given the opportunity, I will defend myself at any time before the whole nation from any such suggestion, no matter from what quarter it may come.

To hold political opponents silent in gaol while a gross untruth is circulated against them is a procedure that cannot be justified to History, even if the moment permits it. Yet, that is the situation that has now been created. It should not have arisen, as our detention was frequently described by the Government as "Preventive"—in contradiction to the allegation that we have done something disloyal to justify Imprisonment. Further, the Prime Minister has himself stated that "he was increasingly sceptical of the existence of a fifth column in this country." But our prolonged imprisonment and the subsequent silence of the Government have since given the unscrupulous and the ignorant an opportunity of which full advantage has been taken.

If we, and through us our dependants, are to suffer not only the miseries but also the stigma of further imprisonment I suggest that, in honour the Government should state publicly whatever they have against us, and that I should at least have the right to make a public reply. I take the entire responsibility for the policy of British Union. All my actions and principles I am prepared at any time to defend publicly before my fellow countrymen.

Tomorrow We Live

by

Oswald Mosley

Introduction

A BOOK of thirty-four thousand words can serve the reader only as an introduction to the spirit and policy of British Union.

The subject is too great to be confined in all detail within such limits of space. But the reader who inquires further will discover in the publications of the British Union an amplitude of detail on every subject of the day. Books and pamphlets by my colleagues, whose range of abilities now cover every sphere of national life, will meet any inquiry, and further detail on some topics can be found in my own books, "The Greater Britain" and "100 Questions Answered."

In these pages the reader will discover, with the exception of the chapter on Foreign Affairs, a policy suited to the character of this country and no other. British Union in whole character is a British principle suited to Britain alone. It is true that our National Socialist and Fascist creed is universal, in different form and method, to all great countries of the modern world. That was true also in their own period of every great creed, political or religious, that our country has ever known. The only difference in this respect between British Union and the old parties is that our creed belongs to the twentieth century, and their creeds to the past that conceived them. But a greater difference arises from the fact that National Socialism and Fascism is in essence a national doctrine which finds in each great nation a character, policy, form and method suited to each particular country. For this reason a far greater divergence will be found in the expression and method of the modern Movement in different countries than prevailed in the case of the international creeds of the past such as Liberalism and Socialism, or Conservatism, which, under various names, can be found in every country in the world.

So the reader will find in these pages a policy born only of British inspiration, and a character and method suited to Britain alone. He will be able to judge for himself our claim for British Union that in constructive conception our policy already far transcends any previous emanation of the modern Movement. We do not borrow ideas from foreign countries and we have no "models" abroad for a plain and simple reason. We are proud enough of our own people to believe that once Britain is awake our people will not follow, but will lead mankind. In this deep faith we hold that no lesser destiny is worthy of the British people than that the whole world shall find in Britain an example. The aim of British Union is no less than this.

Oswald Mosley

System of Government – What is Wrong ?

Financial Democracy

THE will of the people shall prevail. The policy for which the people have voted shall be carried out. This is the essence of good government in an enlightened age. This is the principle which is denied by the system misnamed democracy, which in degeneration is more appropriately called financial democracy. The reason is that government is paralysed by the maintenance of a parliamentary system a century out of date. When the Government elected by the people is incapable of rapid and effective action private and vested interests assume the real power of Government, not by vote or permission of the people, but by power of money dubiously acquired.

In recent years the trifling measures which have struggled through parliamentary obstruction have been insignificant in their effect on the lives of the people by comparison with the immense exercise of money power. Decisions and movements of international finance on Wall Street, and its sub-branch in the City of London, may send prices soaring to create a speculator's paradise at the expense of the real wages of the people, or may send prices crashing to throw millions into unemployment as the aftermath of some gigantic gamble. In terms of the things that really matter to the people, such as real wages, employment, the hours of labour, food prices, and the simple ability to pay the rent, finance, under the present system, can affect the lives of the mass of the people more closely and more terribly in the decision of one afternoon than can Parliament, with puny labour and the mock heroics of sham battles, in the course of a decade. For the instrument of the money power was designed to fit present conditions and to exploit the decadence of an obsolete system. Parliament, on the other hand, was created long before modern conditions existed to meet an altogether different set of facts.

New Conditions

Parliamentary Government, practically in modern form, was designed primarily to prevent the abuse of elementary liberties in a relatively simple rural community with a primitive national economy. The facts of that age have no relation to the periods of steam and power, which were followed swiftly by vast accumulations of finance capital that possess the unlimited international mobility of a world force. Is it really likely that the parliamentary instrument of a century or more ago should be equally suitable to meet the facts of an age which science has revolutionised? Yet on the assumption that the system of government alone required no change, during the century of most startling change that mankind has known, rests the policy and the philosophy of every one of the old parties of the State, Conservative, Liberal and Labour alike!

This patent fallacy which all the old parties teach the people admirably suits the financial exploiter. A parliamentary system devised to check personal outrages by medieval courts or nobles is represented still as the effective guardian of liberty in this age of international finance. It would be as true to say that the bow and arrow with which primitive man defended his farm from the marauding wolf is equally effective to defend him against the tanks of a modern invading army. But the people are persuaded that the instruments by which they preserved some semblance of liberty in the past are still effective to preserve their liberties in modern conditions, in order that these liberties may be taken from them without their loss even being realised.

Parliament and Liberty

It suits our financial masters well that all parties should combine to tell the people that Parliament is the sole effective guardian of liberty, and, naturally, the national Press, which the money power so largely controls, is in unison to echo the same refrain. It is also not surprising to find that anyone who dares to suggest that the liberty of the people alone can be preserved, and their will alone can be carried out, by the entrusting of the Government, which they have elected, with power in the name of the people to act, should be unanimously denounced by the old parties and by the financial Press as a tyrant who desires to overthrow British liberty. As long as the people can be gulled into the belief that they are free today so long can their slavery be perpetuated. Therefore, every instrument of the financial tyranny from party machines to national Press is mobilised behind a barrage of money power to resist the simple principle that power belongs to the people alone, and that their power can only be expressed by giving their freely chosen Government the power to act.

That such power in Government does not exist today can scarcely be denied. It is admitted that only two big Bills can be passed through Parliament in the course of a whole year, which means that any effective programme submitted as a pledge of immediate action to the electorate would take more than the lifetime of a generation to carry out.

Under such conditions every election programme becomes a fraudulent prospectus, which, contrary to the experience of business life, carries the most fraudulent not to gaol, but to Downing Street. Every main Bill has four stages of debate on the floor of the House of Commons alone, and in two stages can be debated line by line by a committee of over six hundred people. In such circumstances the ability of the Opposition to obstruct is unlimited, and no measure can in effect reach the Statute Book in face of really determined opposition. The result is that bargain, compromise, and delay completely stultify the programme for which the majority of the people have voted. Yet this is the procedure which we are told "honest" men are prepared to operate, within a system which renders impossible the execution of the promises which they have given to the people, and by means of which they have secured office and power.

The First Duty

On the contrary, we ask whether any honest man or Movement in politics would not make his first proposal and his first duty to create an instrument of Government by which he could carry out the promises he had made and the policy for which the people have voted. Yet all the old parties combine to resist this principle of elementary honesty, and to denounce as the denial of liberty any suggestion to give to the people the first principle of liberty in the actual execution of the policy they desire. As a result the vote becomes ever more meaningless, and fewer people take the trouble to exercise it as they learn by bitter experience that, no matter the party for which they vote, they never by any chance secure the policy for which they have voted. Farcical becomes the parliamentary scene as the people realise that in a dynamic age this system can never deliver the goods, and like all systems in decline the parliamentary mind seems anxious only to produce its own caricature.

In the Light of history it will ever be regarded as a curious and temporary aberration of the human mind that great nations should elect a Government to do a job and should then elect an Opposition to stop them doing it. Fortunately, even in the wildest excesses of this transient mania, this delusion never spread to the business world, and no business man outside an asylum has yet been observed to engage a staff of six to carry on the work of his firm, and then to engage an additional staff of four to stop them doing their job. Curious to posterity will appear the principle of creating at the same time a Government to do the nation's work and an Opposition to frustrate it. But stranger still will seem the final reduction to absurdity of the parliamentary system whereby a Prime Minister is paid £10,000 a year to do the nation's job, and the Leader of the Opposition is paid, and accepts, £2,000 a year of the nation's money to stop him doing it. Yet this extraordinary harlequinade, in which nothing serious, in terms of the modern mind, is ever done, and little serious is even discussed, is today represented as the only means of preserving the liberties of the people.

The instruments by which this great racket has been achieved are plain to see. The first is the maintenance of an obsolete parliamentary system still invested from a past of difficult conditions with the myth of liberty, by means of which Government is paralysed in order that the real power of Government may be exercised elsewhere, not by the chosen of the people but by the chosen of finance. The second instrument is the monopoly of propaganda by the money power in the shape of a Press also invested with the myth of liberty from a past of different conditions. The Free Press built by genuine journalists who were vendors of honest "news" long ago gave place in most of the national Press to the financial combine which acquires control of great blocks of newspaper shares. So the money power again in the name of a Free Press can serve to the people not only the opinions but also the "news" which serves the interests of the money power. Not only are our "free" British denied any meaning to the vote in the shape of ever getting what they want, but they are also denied even the small privilege of learning the truth. For power and propaganda alike are in the hands of a force whose interests conflict with the interests of the people and is careful that they should not even learn the truth. Thus the myth of freedom in Parliament and Press combine to promote the slavery of the people.

Finance Power

Most of the Press is owned outright by the money power, or is controlled by the advertisements which money power controls, and Parliament is paralysed by talk that power may reside elsewhere. But the argument may be taken further, for the economic system which is maintained by finance power for the benefit of its own interests, and to the detriment of every interest of the people, also ensures that any Government may at any time be broken by the money power. The international economic system is supported by every party of the State, Conservative, Liberal and Labour alike. It will be shown in detail in chapter three of this book that this system enables any Government to be broken at any time by the financial power, as the weak Socialist Government was broken in Britain in 1931, and the weak Socialist Government of Blum was broken in France in 1937.

It was not enough for finance to dope the system of Government with the talkative parliamentary system of a century ago. Finance in the economic system also retains the power at any time to knock a Government on the head. By way of further precaution the finance of the money power controls the party machines, which in their turn control Parliament and Government.

So this is finality in the land of "liberty and free speech":

1. Government is paralysed by the system of talk that power may reside elsewhere;

2. Government can at any time be destroyed by the power of money alone;

3. the Press which controls opinion is itself largely controlled by the money power;

4. the party machines which control even the right of the individual to make a speech to an appreciable audience in public are also controlled by the money power.

So what is left to you "free Britons" to voice your opinion and make your will effective? You can go into a public-house and grumble in the assurance that no one will take the slightest notice of what you say. But even then you must be sure to be out in the streets by closing time, because the Old Woman of Westminster prefers, even in your private life, to treat you as a child rather than as a man.

There stands the Briton in the street, gulled into the acceptance of slavery by words about liberty, and boasting of freedom, while in truth denied the freedom to call his own even the soul of which alone his masters have not robbed him, for the simple reason that it has no cash value.

Is that really the Briton - tricked, fooled, hagridden, exploited, enslaved? Or does a generation arise again, breaking from the hands of manhood resurgent the fetters of decadence and seeing with the ardent eyes of an awakened giant the land that they shall make their own.

British Union System Of Government

British Union Movement

THE will of the people shall prevail. The policy for which the people have voted shall be carried out. This is the essence of British Union Government. In the previous chapter the present complete frustration of the people's will has been examined and the formidable instruments of that frustration have been surveyed. In cold fact the money power commands Government, Parliament, Party Machinery and Press. Not only does it possess the power to render Government impotent and, if necessary, to break Government; money power also possesses the means of preventing any new opinion or even any true news from reaching the people at all. Faced with this formidable power and almost limitless corruption of a decadent system, those who founded the British Union were moved by the deep belief that from the people themselves alone could be created the instrument by which freedom could be won for the people, and by which our country could be redeemed to greatness. Such an instrument clearly, in its whole character and structure, must differ from the old parties of the State.

It would be idle with infinite labour to create a new movement to combat current corruption of such a loose and flaccid character that, like the revolutionary movements of the immediate past, it would fall an easy victim to the very corruption that it was designed to destroy. If this basic principle is understood, much in the history and character of our Movement that has been misunderstood will be easily comprehended. We had to create an "instrument of steel" because we know from our experience of democracy that any character less hard and tested would easily succumb to the system that it was designed to combat.

Consequently our Movement has rested from the outset upon the principles of struggle, sacrifice, and voluntary discipline. In the fire of that struggle and by the force of the sacrifice for which I have never called in vain, the "instrument of steel" has been forged that shall cut through corruption to a larger freedom than this land has ever known.

It has been forged from the heart and soul of the people alone in the sacrifice of thousands of unknown but utterly devoted men and women who have been ready to give all that Britain might live.

This Movement has been created by simple people in face of money power, party power, and press power without any aid from the great names of the present system, and in face of every weapon of boycott and misrepresentation that the money power could mobilise. Thus ever have been born the great determinist forces of history in face of all material things by the force of the spirit alone.

So has been accomplished the first stage in the mission of regeneration which is the creation from the people themselves and from the people alone of a Movement capable of leading the mass of the people to freedom. Those who sacrifice all for an undying cause are inevitably a minority even in the movement they create. Soon thousands came and now come who are gladly welcomed to give support or any kind of service, but many of whom for innumerable reasons, domestic and business, are inhibited from the supreme sacrifice that builds this Movement. Still later a whole nation will give support with enthusiasm to a cause that has been built through the sacrifice by pioneers of most that makes life dear to men.

But they who lead the people to a higher civilisation are ever those who are capable of supreme self dedication. The authority of leadership carries with it the responsibility of such a life. Thus our new leaders of the people in every area of the land have been discovered, tried, and tested in the actual ordeal of struggle.

Their sacrifice during a struggle harder and fiercer in its whole nature than any movement has known before in this country is the guarantee to the people that they will not again be betrayed. Men and women do not sacrifice all in order to betray the thing to which they have given their lives. A Fascist who, in power after such a struggle, betrayed his cause, would betray his own life blood. Thus the struggle of a National Socialist Movement is a necessary preliminary to the exercise of power, because the bitter character of that struggle gives to the people an absolute guarantee that those who have passed through that test unbroken will not betray their people or their country. Thus alone is forged the "instrument of steel" to save and then to serve the people.

The Leadership Principle

The rebirth of a nation comes from the people in a clear and ordered sequence. The People, their Movement, their Government, their Power. To create their Government and to overthrow the Government of the money power which oppresses them the people have first to create their Movement. This act enables them for the first time to give meaning to the vote by electing their Government to power. The final stage is to arm this Government with power in their name to act.

To represent this process as the constitution of a dictatorship against the will of the people is a travesty of the facts as dishonest as it is childish. The only dictatorship that we propose for this country is the dictatorship of the people themselves, which shall replace the present dictatorship of the vested interests. Our Movement offers to the people not dictatorship but leadership through an instrument by which their will can be carried out. British Union and leadership seek not to be dictator to the people but servant of the people.

The only stipulation that we make is the simple condition that if the people want us to do the job they shall give us the power to do it. Is that unreasonable? Is it not a waste of the people's time and money to create a Government which has not the power to act? Is it not simple dishonesty for any man or movement to accept office without the power to act and without the ability to perform what he has undertaken to do?

Our principle is the leadership principle which has nothing whatever to do with dictatorship. It is true that this principle is the opposite to the collective irresponsibility of the "democratic" committee system but that does not make it dictatorship. British Union believes in the following simple principles: (1) give a man a job to do; (2) give him the power to do it; (3) hold him responsible for doing it; (4) sack him if he does not do it. Our principles, therefore, are neither dictatorship nor the fugitive irresponsibility of a committee. We have seen the committee system in action within financial democracy and have observed its consequence. If several men are in name responsible no one is, in fact, responsible, and no one can be held to account for failure.

Everyone shelters behind his colleagues and disclaims personal responsibility; all wanted to do the right thing, but none could persuade their colleagues to do it. Not only does the committee system of financial democracy dissipate action in endless talk; it breeds cowardice and evasion in leadership in place of courage and responsibility. Therefore, in the building of our Movement and in the building of a Government we believe in the leadership principle, which means personal and individual responsibility.

Whether a man occupies a position of minor responsibility or a position of the gravest responsibility in the State that task is his responsibility and that of no other, and for the execution of that task he shall be held responsible to the people. Authority can never be divided because divided authority means divided responsibility, and that leads to the futility and cowardice of the committee system. Failure to comprehend this principle is failure alike to understand the principles of National Socialism or the essence of any creed of dynamic action and achievement since the world began. But to represent as dictatorship authority freely conferred by the people in return for the manly acceptance of personal responsibility is a misunderstanding, or rather misrepresentation, equally gross.

In the building of our Movement and the creation of our Government the principle is leadership, and not dictatorship, for plain and obvious reasons. No one can be compelled to join our Movement and any member can walk out of it any day he likes if he does not accept its principles or leadership. He is perfectly free to try to do better himself in the creation and conduct of another movement. In this country, as in others, many tried their hand until the confusion of little societies with imitative policies and inflated egotisms faded away in the advance of British Union to be a National Movement, by the simple test of alone possessing the capacity to attract a national following. It is idle, therefore, to argue that prior to the winning of power our Movement rests on the dictatorship principle for none need belong to it who do not wish. After the winning of power equally it rests not on dictatorship but on the leadership principle, for power is conferred by the free vote of the people and can be removed by the free vote of the people.

The Structure of Government

British Union seeks power by the vote of the people alone at a general election. But we tell the people quite frankly in advance that we will not accept responsibility without power, because we believe it to be dishonest to take office without the ability to carry out the policy for which the people have voted. The first measure of British Union Government will, therefore, be a General Powers Bill conferring on Government the means to act by order, subject to the right of Parliament elected by the vote of the people at any time to dismiss the Government by vote of censure if it abuses power. Subject to this right of dismissal by Parliament the Government will be free to act without delay or obstruction from the interminable rigmarole of present parliamentary procedure. Parliament will be called together at regular intervals to review the work of the Government and to criticise and suggest. M.P.s will be armed with facts for criticism and suggestion which they do not at present possess, because they will not spend most of their time in the corrupting atmosphere of Westminster but in the stimulating atmosphere of their own constituencies among the people whom they represent. In particular British Union will give most of the M.P.s an executive task in place of a purely talkative role in a complete reform of the local authority system. Local authority areas will be enlarged and all purely local matters will be delegated to their jurisdiction. Again, the leadership principle will be employed and the executive leader of the local authority will be an M.P. of the majority party in Parliament elected from the area over whose local authority he presides. He will be advised and assisted by a local Council elected on the principle of occupational franchise, the method of which both local and national will be described later in this chapter. Each member of the Council will be an executive officer in charge of a Local Government department and responsible to the local leader, who will be responsible to the Government of the nation. Thus committee irresponsibility in local, as in national affairs, will yield place to the leadership principle of personal responsibility and effective action.

Local leaders both in the first Parliament of British Union and in the permanent system will be selected from the Movement for which the majority of the people have voted. To many this may seem a revolutionary principle but, in fact, is it not plain common sense? Local leaders will be selected as ministers are today from the party for which the majority of the country have voted and will be given power to act. Can Government ever be effective or action ever be taken if differing policies are pursued by National Government and local authority? What would happen to a business whose head office pursued one policy and whose branch offices pursued another? Can any real democrat object to the principle that the programme for which the majority of the people have voted shall be carried out both nationally and locally? We hear so much these days of the rights of the minority that many are inclined to forget the rights of the majority. Is it democracy or any form of free government for the majority of the people to vote for a programme which is completely frustrated not only by obstruction at Westminster but by minority obstruction also in hundreds of different and conflicting local Councils? In practice financial democracy means that in the name of minority rights the right of the majority is invariably denied. British Union policy rests on the simple principle that nationally and locally the will of the majority of the people shall prevail. The incidental advantage of the execution of this principle is that the majority of M.P.s are saved from the demoralising chatter of the House of Commons lobbies and given an executive task with personal responsibility that will evoke from the people's representatives the capacities requisite to a man of action. No process is more necessary to the creation of effective government than to transmute the people's representatives from mere talkers into men of action.

Many a good revolutionary has arrived at Westminster roaring like a lion, only a few months later to be cooing as the tame dove of his opponents. The bar, the smoking room, the lobby, the dinner tables of his constituents' enemies, and the "atmosphere of the best club in the country," very quickly rob a people's champion of his vitality and fighting power. Revolutionary movements lose their revolutionary ardour as a result long before they ever reach power, and the warrior of the platform becomes the lapdog of the lobbies. In the light of this experience British Union M.P.s from the outset will go to Westminster under solemn pledge not to mix socially, or even to speak, to their opponents. They will go to Parliament to fight for the people who sent them there, and not to fraternise with men who have betrayed the people.

Thus only with sustained fighting spirit and revolutionary ardour can the nation's cause be served. In Westminster, as outside, British Union must be the "instrument of steel" in the service of the people. Until we win power we shall fight every inch of the way, and directly upon the winning of power we shall establish an instrument of Government capable of executing the people's will. This instrument, nationally and locally, will be created by the vote of the majority of the people and this instrument, nationally and locally, will execute their will. Power conferred by the people in their name will be exercised, and that power shall be removed by the vote of the people alone, to whom alone, under the Crown, we will account and be responsible.

Occupational Franchise

We have observed that in the first Parliament of British Union complete power of action by Government is combined with the right of Parliament elected by the people to dismiss the Government if it abuses power. Government's power of action nationally and locally is complete, but so also the control of the people over Government is complete.

We come now to the consideration of the permanent system which is created with the second Parliament of British Union. The first Parliament, by necessity, is elected on the existing franchise which is geographical. That franchise is a relic of the past, in which the interests of men and women were more centred in their locality of residence than in their occupation within the national economy. Such conditions have long passed away as the main categories of occupation assumed a national in place of a purely local character. Today the fact that a man is an engineer or doctor, a farmer or cotton operative, is a greater factor in his existence than the particular locality in which he happens to reside. In modern and scientific organisation occupation definitely supersedes in importance the chance of residence. In geographical constituencies thousands of diverse human beings and interests are fortuitously brought together by the franchise without much knowledge of each other and with few interests in common. Again this system of voting in its obsolescence produces the abuses of decay.

Early electorates of a less complex age could discriminate in giving a vote on simple national issues for one or other local leader whose character and views were well known to them. An election with the vast modern electorate is a very different matter as the great network of national questions is far too complex for any but whole time specialists thoroughly to understand, and the personalities and real views of the candidates can only be known at all to a fraction of the voters. The confusion of a present election under the old system lends itself to the charlatan candidate employing the catchword of the moment without any relation either to the reality of national issues or to the policies which he subsequently supports in Parliament. In such circumstances the slick talker generally defeats the serious worker, and the divorce between promise and subsequent performance leads increasingly to the Wholesale disillusion of the electorate.

It is, therefore, necessary to restore not only reality but understanding to the vote. The idea that all men on all subjects are equally competent to give a verdict becomes, in modern conditions, an ever more manifest absurdity. Therefore, we propose an occupational franchise that men and women may vote on problems they well understand for personnel with whom they have a long familiarity.

Men and women will vote not as residents in a particular locality but as persons engaged in a particular occupation. Doctors will vote as doctors, engineers as engineers, miners as miners, farmers as farmers, farm workers as farm workers, married women as housewives and mothers with a franchise of their own.

Women's Part

It is noteworthy today that the mothers of the nation possess few representatives in Parliament with any special competence to represent them. Women's questions are usually handled by ageing spinsters, for the simple reason that most women with any practical experience of maternity find the conflict between home and public life so intolerable that they retire again to a sphere where their true interests lie. The problem can only be resolved by occupational franchise, which gives them special representation in a Parliament that will not remove them altogether from the interests they represent.

The care of the mother and the child is one of the main neglects of the present system and will be among the main concerns of British Union. It is only right, therefore, that this great interest should secure proper representation with the other great interests of the nation. This does not mean that we seek to relegate women purely to the home, which is a charge denied in practice by the act that we present today a larger proportion of women candidates to the electorate than any other party. In our permanent system women in industry or the professions will have their vote and their representatives within their occupation. An economic system which provides work for all has no need to drive women from industry. But a political system which guards the health and strength of the race will certainly prevent the grave scandal of women being driven from the home against their will because the miserable wages of the men cannot keep the home together. Women, whether in home or industry, will hold a high and honoured place in accord with British tradition and will receive full measure of representation and weight in the counsels of the State.

End of the Party Game

Occupational franchise, therefore, will secure a technical Parliament suited to the problems of a technical age. A vote given with full information and, consequently, with a sense of responsibility will secure a serious and dignified assembly. Such a Parliament will consider national questions freely on their merits and not beneath the lash of the party whip in the ignoble scramble for place which has become the hallmark of present politics. It is clear that such a system brings to an end the party game and apart from other advantages it is deliberately designed to that end. British Union means to bring to an end the party game. There is no time in the modern world, with menacing problems of a dynamic age for mere opposition for the sake of opposing, in the hope of getting the other man's job by the simple process of blacking his face by any means, fair or foul.

Under our system a man or woman will be elected because he, or she, is a good engineer or a good doctor, not a party doctor or party engineer. The M.P. will emerge to prominence and office not by dexterity in mere debate, or by bibulous capacity to sit up all night to obstruct the business of the nation, but by serious criticism and constructive suggestion which will make real contribution to the deliberations of the nation. In a new age the party type will pass, together with the corruption of the party machine.

People's Control Over Government

Few will deny that the constructive seriousness of such a Parliament will be an improvement on the frivolity and chicanery of an obsolete system. But the question is often raised how, in the absence of organised opposition, the people can change the Government if they wish. The answer is that in the permanent system of British Union the life of the Government will depend on the direct vote of the people, held at regular and frequent intervals. If the people wish to change the Government the simple remedy is to vote against it. In the event of an adverse vote the Crown, to which British Union is entirely loyal, will intervene, and H.M. the King, in the restoration of his full historic prerogative, will send for new ministers who in his opinion have a good chance of receiving the support of the country at a fresh vote. Thus in the permanent system of British Union nothing intervenes between Government and people. No log rolling in Parliament or intrigue in the lobby can shake the power of Government. The will of the people and that alone can make and break the Government.

Opposition Parties

But the "democrat" at this point usually expostulates that the people cannot decide to vote against a Government if no opposition parties exist organised for party warfare. Surely of all the insults which financial democracy offers to the intelligence of the electorate this is the gravest. Are we really to believe that a great people cannot make up their mind that they do not like a Government, and give a vote to that effect, without a lot of little politicians bawling in their ears that they do not like it, and asking them to vote for a dozen confused and contradictory policies. The suggestion that a great nation cannot live without professional politicians is an insult alike to their intelligence and their temper. Yet the "democratic politicians " who pretend that the people are capable, without such advice, of giving a decision on the broad issue of whether they want a Government or not, are at pains to defend the present system, which rests on the grotesque assumption that every elector understands every national question ranging from currency reform and naval strategy to the price of beer.

The facts are surely at complete variance with the pretensions of financial democracy. The people are perfectly competent to give a verdict on the general conduct of Government without any assistance from a bawling match of politicians. The elector also is perfectly competent to elect a Parliament to deal with the technical problems of the modern age, provided he votes within his own occupation on problems and for personnel that he thoroughly understands. But in plain terms of commonsense the engineer or the doctor finds it a bad joke for his particular problems to be settled by a vast majority of the electorate who have not the slightest acquaintance with those problems.

We are faced with the necessity of combining the right of the people to control and dismiss Government with serious discussion of highly complicated and diverse problems. The solution of British Union is to give the people direct control over Government by direct vote of the whole nation at regular intervals, when they will give their verdict on the general issue whether Government is good or bad, and, at the same time, to give them a separate occupational franchise for the election of a serious and modern Parliament on which Government will rely for the detailed consideration of modern problems.

With this solution we challenge the present system of financial democracy which in theory rests on the absurd assumption that everyone understands everything. In practice it results in such complete confusion that the great interests can govern under cover of the all-pervading smoke screen, and the great rogues of finance can get away with their booty, while the antics of the little kept politicians distract the attention of the people from reality.

A Government resting on the direct vote of the people and a Parliament elected by the informed vote of the people reconciles freedom with action and lays the foundation of the modern State.

The House of Lords

The present House of Lords can find no place in a modern system and will be abolished by British Union. It will be replaced by a new Second Chamber which reconciles British tradition with modern Government. That Chamber will represent the proved ability and experience of the nation. It will comprise industrial representatives from the National Council of Corporations, representatives of all the main religious denominations, representatives of education, representatives of the Services and men and women automatically appointed by their long occupation of positions of conspicuous service to the State. From such an assembly of personal experience and ability Government can draw great reserves of capacity for advice and constructive suggestion in all the multifarious variety of modern problems. This conception also carries out in modern form the original aim of the British Constitution. The House of Lords was constructed to represent the industrial, cultural, and spiritual aspects of the national life. In those days agriculture was the only industry and the peers owned most of the land. Today agriculture is not the only industry and most peers have little to do with the land, while even the most ardent defender of the House of Lords will not claim that the peers are today the sole repositories of national culture.

The present House of Lords, therefore, no longer executes the original idea of the Constitution and is an anachronism. British Union will implement that original British tradition by giving to the Second Chamber a character really representative of the industrial, cultural and spiritual life of the nation. In the latter sphere it is only right that in an enlightened age the religious beliefs of all the main sections of our fellow citizens should be represented. In practice as well as in theory British Union believes in religious toleration, and that belief will be implemented by the representation of all denominations.

Freedom of the Individual - The Press

It remains to consider the effect on the individual of this structure of Government in terms of human freedom and the full individual life. If we accept the premise that economic freedom is the only true basis of individual freedom in modern conditions it must be agreed that effective power of action in Government is the prerequisite of individual freedom. For such power of action is necessary to bring to an end the economic chaos which today robs the individual of economic liberty in an age from which science can win this boon for all. But some still shrink from the only means of securing the larger economic liberty for the people through fear that the process will deprive them of a "political liberty" which in fact does not today exist. This type can find no answer in practical detail to the simple query, when have they ever got anything for which they have voted? They are baffled completely by the further question, what is the use of a "political liberty" which has never yet brought them any practical result? So they usually fall back on vague generalities concerning the inestimable boons of freedom of speech and freedom of the Press."

British Union System Of Government

It is, therefore, necessary to examine in a little detail in what freedom of Press and speech today consists, and what would be the position of these "principles" under British Union Government. It may at once be stated categorically, to the surprise of many, that the freedom of the individual in these respects will be far greater than it is today. What freedom of the Press does the individual possess today? He certainly does not possess the freedom to secure the printing in the Press of either news or views which do not suit the interests of the Press. In the national Press, at any rate, he may not even humbly creep into back page correspondence columns if his opinions be regarded as in any way dangerous.

What prospect has the individual of founding a national newspaper of his own in conditions where monopoly has reached the point that no newcomer can hope to make good unless he can command millions of capital? A man of relatively moderate capital resources may possibly acquire control of a local paper of purely local influence or even, by a lifetime of hard work, may build such a modest influence in the State by genuine journalism without much capital resources. But no other save the great finance powers can now arrive in the national Press in modern monopoly conditions. So, in fact, when our opponents speak of the freedom of the Press they mean the power of the great financiers to purvey their opinions and their news to the people, with scant reference to the merits of the journalism, but with much reference to the weight of money power, which enables them to purchase circulations by canvass and free gifts, for which the advertisements of the great interests alone can recompense them.

The national Press, in fact, long since has become a matter not of journalism but of finance. In such circumstances what transparent mockery it is to tell the individual that he possesses freedom of opinion and of Press, for he, too, can start a newspaper. It is equivalent to the alleged statement of the classic Tory that Britain was a free country because rich or poor alike were free to sleep on the Embankment.

91

Free Speech

As for freedom of speech, in what today does it consist? It is true that anyone can carry a soap box to a street corner and from that eminence may make any moderate noise that he sees fit to emit, unless the whim of the local police chief transports him on charge of obstruction before a bench of magistrates selected for other political qualifications than street corner oratory. But may we not assume as the premise of the argument that none but a purely "mental" type desires to talk under these conditions purely for the sake of talking without any effective action following from his words? Judged by that criterion of reality, freedom of speech does not exist. For the persuasion of our countrymen is meaningless unless we can persuade them to do something. That power does not exist without a party machine to mobilise their votes, and party machines are not the possessions of individuals but of the great interests.

Freedom of speech for the individual is confined to the "mental" type who enjoys indefinitely a fruitless exercise of his lungs at a street corner without the slightest prospect of his words ever being translated into action. In fact, "freedom of speech" under financial democracy is merely another solemn make believe which obscures the reality of tyranny. No individual has any hope of producing any practical effect by words unless he serves one of the great party machines and, as we shall observe in the next chapter, the party machines in their turn serve the great interests and by the very nature of the system which they support are inevitably the servants of finance. So in actual practice under this system freedom of speech is the freedom to be the servant of the financier.

To this the retort may be made that any individual is free to win the support of his fellow countrymen, and in so doing from their enthusiasm to create his own machine in face of the money power. To that argument in turn we make the proud reply that this phenomenon has been achieved but once in post war Britain in the creation of British Union. And, the writer may add a note from that unique experience at the end of some years of such a struggle; if anyone believes that it is an easy and everyday task to create a new Movement from nothing by the force of the spirit alone in face of Money Power, Press power and Party power, he is welcome to the unparalleled exertion of that experience, but he will win success only at the cost of something in his own life and being that is not an everyday occasion.

Real Freedom of Press and Speech

In face of the present negation of freedom in the realm of Press and speech, British Union approaches a constructive solution in the determination to win real freedom of Press and speech for the people. That freedom will rest on two main principles: (1) that freedom of Press means the freedom of the people to read the truth in the national Press and not the freedom of finance power to tell lies to the people in support of vested interests; (2) that freedom of speech for the individual means an effective method of translating his opinion into action if by words he can persuade sufficient of his fellows to agree with him. In the sphere of the Press, therefore, we lay down the truly revolutionary principle that the Press shall tell the truth. To this end the proprietors of great newspapers will be liable to prosecution if it can be proved in Court that they have published news which is not true, and the penalty will be particularly severe if it can be shown that such Publication was deliberately and maliciously conceived in support of a private interest to the detriment of the national interest. It is a curious anomaly of present confusion that an individual who is libelled can obtain redress from the law but the nation when libelled can obtain no redress. Therefore, it will be open to a Government, elected by the people, on behalf of the nation to sue a newspaper proprietor if his paper publishes facts which are false to the detriment of the nation's interest, particularly if the object is to promote a private interest at the nation's expense. This will curtail the freedom of the Press to publish news which is untrue, but it will confer upon the people the freedom to read news which is true.

British Union takes the simple view that the freedom of the people to learn the truth should supersede the freedom of the vested interest to deceive the people. For this reason our new "freedom of the Press" rests on the simple but revolutionary principle that the Press shall tell the truth. Consequently neither national nor local paper which tells the truth will in any way be affected, and no proprietor can have any complaint unless he makes the unexpected admission that he is in the habit of not telling the truth in his papers at present.

Some organs of the national Press no doubt will pass unscathed through this test and certainly the great majority of our local papers. For local papers, on the whole, are straightforward purveyors of news, serving their localities as honest journalists who give a fair representation to all opinions, with a responsible regard to national interests.

If the whole national Press was conducted in the same method and in the same spirit as the majority of the local Press they would have nothing to fear from British Union Government.

Free Speech and Corporate Life

The machinery for putting into practice the principle of freedom of speech is equally definite. We start from the premise that if freedom of speech is to be a reality the individual must possess effective means of translating words into actions. To this end any individual with industry, interest, or profession, will be invited to enter into the appropriate Corporation, the detailed structure of which is suggested in Mr. Raven Thomson's able book on this subject and will not here be repeated beyond a survey of economic function in Chapter 4. Within the Corporation every one is not only permitted but by every means encouraged to express opinions both constructive and critical, and is provided with a means of making opinion effective. For if the individual can move the relevant Corporation by argument that Corporation's opinion, representing a very substantial factor in the State, is transmitted to Government, and for Government to ignore Corporate opinion would be to court dismissal at the next vote on universal franchise by the sum of individual voters who comprise the Corporations.

The mechanism of the Corporation, ready to the hand of the individual, is a more powerful instrument for the expression of free speech in effective terms of reality than the lonely and meaningless pedestal of the street corner orator. Through Corporate life the individual wins meaning and reality for freedom of speech. Such real and effective freedom of speech is a basic necessity for British Union Government which in the achievement of a revolution in national life must ever carry the people with it, and maintain a far closer contact with the people's opinion than Government possesses today.

It is good enough for the Governments of financial democracy to consult the people in a mock election once in five years in the hope that they will go to sleep in the interval so that Government can go to sleep as well. That is a procedure possible for Governments which in reality only exist to preserve the existing system and to guard its vested interests. But such a conception is not good enough for a revolutionary Movement determined to wrest from chaos a nobler civilisation. For such an achievement it is not enough to obtain the tacit consent of the people, it is necessary to carry the people with us all the way and all the time on the march to higher things. That is why we must know all the time what they are feeling and thinking and have precise means to that end. That is why we must devise machinery not only to give the people freedom of speech but to make that freedom effective. Contact between Government and people must ever be so close that the flame of our own revolutionary passion may pass continually from the souls of pioneers to fire and maintain the spirit of the people at a white heat of ardour unknown to the doped and tepid supporters of financial democracy.

For this shall be a great comradeship between the people and the Government they have elected to lead them. They must ever know what we are doing and we must ever know what they are thinking. That is why we believe in the people's real freedom of speech and will win it for them. Thus only can be secured that close and sacred union between the people and their Government by which alone a great nation shall march again to greatness.

Economic System – What Is Wrong ?

Economics of Poverty or Plenty

THE economic system is breaking down for reasons that are plain to see. But these reasons are never seriously discussed in Press or Parliament because the decadence of an economic System suits well the money power which controls Press and Parliament. Realisation by the people of the reasons for economic breakdown means the end of finance power. Therefore, every reason other than the plain and true reason must be provided, and every difficulty must be represented as temporary and transient rather than fundamental and inherent to a system in decline.

Every boom of the present system grows shorter and lesser; every depression grows deeper and longer. The crazy machine of the present economy rocks ever more violently toward a final disaster. The plain and simple reason is that the economic system is a century out of date. That system is the international system of trade and that system is responsible both for the evils and for the danger of the present time. In the sphere of economics, even more than in the sphere of Government, it should be clear that the method which grew from the facts of a century ago is not designed to meet the facts of today. The economic system was born of the age of poverty economics; we live in the age of plenty economics.

The facts are precisely the opposite to a century ago; yet the system in all fundamentals is precisely the same and the attitude of the parties is the same. To the international parties everything that has happened in the interval might never have occurred. The arrival of the technician, the introduction of the age of steam and later the age of power has altered for ever the economic environment of mankind. Yet all parties, including the Labour Party, support the international system of trade which preceded this vast revolution in fact and circumstance.

At the beginning of the international system the world was faced with the problem of poverty. Mankind could with difficulty produce enough to live. So it was argued with force by the economists of the period that each nation should produce what it was best fitted by nature to produce, judged by the sole criterion of cheapness, and should exchange such products with corresponding products from other nations. It was further argued that any barrier cutting across the thin trickle of international trade would universally diminish the standard of life, and in ensuing chaos might even result in the return of man to a primitive agricultural existence from which he had so recently struggled. It is unnecessary to discuss the merits of the arguments for or against that theory, though in retrospect we may condemn strongly the sacrifice of British agriculture to the extremes of that conception. It is redundant to discuss in modern times that theory because the whole premise on which it rested has been destroyed. It was born of the age of poverty, in which the question of the hour was how to produce enough to live.

This is the age of plenty, in which the question of the hour is how to sell what we can produce. The facts and the problem are exactly the opposite but the system and the parties remain the same. From all parties, platforms and Press we hear, in varying language and degree, insistence upon the maintenance and restoration of international trade and the free exchange of goods between nations. The main object of their denunciation is "economic nationalism," by which they mean any suggestion for nations themselves to produce as large a quantity as possible of the goods that they consume. Yet none can deny that every great nation today, with the aid of modern science, is itself capable of producing in almost unlimited quantity practically every commodity it requires, provided it has access to raw materials.

In face of all fact the politicians maintain a system that rests on the assumption that mankind can only with difficulty produce enough to live, and that goods must, therefore, be produced only by nations particularly suited to produce them and freely exchanged between nations. On the other hand, every technician and engineer knows that in modern conditions any great nation can turn out with mass production all essential commodities, provided it possesses skilled labour, machinery and raw materials.

In fact, the old parties all support a system resting on an assumption of facts which the thousands of technicians over whom they rule well know to be nonsense. Facts may change in gigantic revolutions of science but the politician changes never. This is not because he is so stupid as he appears but because, for a reason we shall study later, a system of decadence suits his masters better than a system which functions for the welfare of the people.

Export Trade

So our unfortunate industry is compelled to serve the international system and at all costs to national economy to fight for the export trade on which that system rests. In the battle for exports modern science and modern condition has again confronted our trade with an entirely new set of facts which have built such insuperable obstacles that the fight for exports ever since the war has been a steadily losing battle. The spread of modern science and technique has enabled our former customers to industrialise themselves. These new foreign industries are protected not by the obsolete weapon of tariffs but by barriers of complete exclusion which have not yet been lowered in response to the pious requests of British statesmanship, at innumerable international conferences, that these foreign nations should ruin their own industries in order to provide us with the markets that we lack. In remaining markets still open to us we are faced with a competition, unprecedented and irresistible, which has been created by the vile exploitation of modern science by finance power in the industrialisation of the Orient.

Western finance has provided the loans which have equipped the East with equal machinery to the West, and has hired the Western technician to teach the Oriental to perform the simplified tasks of mass production with modern mechanical technique at a third of the wages and for longer hours of monotonous toil that white labour can endure. The result has been a stream of sweated goods undercutting British products or the markets of the world. Their deadly effect can be observed in the cold statistics that show the decline of Lancashire and Yorkshire exports under the attack of rising Japanese exports and the vast increase in Indian sweated products.

Internationalism and the Standard of Life

Not only are we subject to the undercutting of sweated products in the markets of the world. In addition the blessings of the international system permit, despite all pretence at protection, great and increasing quantities of these goods even to invade our home market. British industry is not only being driven by new enemies and new weapons from our world position, but is being counter-attacked as well on the home and still more on the Empire market.

In such circumstances we ask the old parties a simple question that has never yet been answered. How can any international system, whether capitalist or Socialist, advance or even maintain the standard of life of our people? The international system of trade admittedly means the more or less free exchange of goods between nations. How can we raise or even maintain British wages in the face of competition from sweated labour supplied with the same machinery but paid a third of the wages and working for far longer hours? Whether industry be capitalist and owned by the unrestricted individual, or Socialist and owned by the State, how can it function in modern conditions if the system be international? This question is the epitaph of international Socialism, for it drives every thinking Socialist, together with men of all parties, who seriously study modern conditions, into the ranks of British Union, which organises industrial freedom within the insulated boundaries of an Empire economic system.

Purchasing Power

The construction of that system belongs to the next chapter, for the analysis of breakdown must be pursued further to a conclusion. We indict the international system as the root of present evils in the economic sphere. In view of the facts above recited the effect of the international system is plain to observe on the main problem of our day, which is the problem of "purchasing power." Few will deny that the industrial question today is how to sell what we produce. None can deny the truism that to sell one must find customers and, as foreign markets progressively close in the light of export figures over any substantial period, the home customer becomes ever more the outlet of industry. But the home customer is simply the British people, on whose purchasing power our industry is ever more dependent.

For the most part the purchasing power of the British people depends on the wages and salaries that they are paid. Here the effect of the international system on the central problem of purchasing power becomes obvious. The wages and salaries of the British people are held down far below the level which modern science and the potential of production could justify because their labour is subject to the undercutting competition of sweated labour on both foreign and home markets. Again we ask, how can British purchasing power be increased or even maintained in face of such competition? Yet internationalism condemns us to such competition and as a result, while foreign markets close, the purchasing power of the British people remains far inadequate to provide a home market capable of absorbing anything approaching the full production of British industry. The result is the tragic paradox of poverty and unemployment amid potential plenty.

Thousands even in the boom periods of this system, let alone the depressions, walk the streets in unemployment, and machines are idle which are capable of producing the goods that millions require but lack the power to buy. Internationalism, in fact, robs the British people of the power to buy the goods that the British people produce. In final frenzy of this system, with accompanying mumbo jumbo from the witch doctors of its economics, the people are even taught to believe that some mystic virtue resides in goods exported for foreign consumption, but that no good can come of the production of goods by Britons for the benefit of Britons.

Rationalisation

In economic result every blessing with which science now endows mankind becomes in practice a curse. The rationalisation of industry with higher wealth potential should be the greatest benefit of the period. In fact, it is dreaded by the people because it brings ever increasing unemployment with every increase in the power to produce. The reason again is plain to see because each increase in the power to produce goods is not accompanied by a corresponding increase in the power to consume goods. On the contrary, because internationalism restricts purchasing power rationalisation results in a lesser rather than a greater power to consume the wealth that it produces. Rationalisation enables industry either to produce more goods with the same amount of labour, or to produce the same amount of goods with less labour. Because the purchasing power of the people is held down by the unfair competition of the international system purchasing power cannot increase at the same time that rationalisation increases the power to produce. As a result only the same amount of goods as before can be produced after rationalisation, and they are produced with less labour. More are thrown, with loss of wages, on to the scrap heap of unemployment, and purchasing power is further diminished just at the moment it is essential that it should be increased if the victory of science is to be a blessing and not a curse.

Labour and Inflation

With the millstone of internationalism round their necks the old parties are incapable of dealing with the central problem of purchasing power. They are inhibited from the only solution of building up British wages to provide, by higher purchasing power, a greater market for British products, because higher wages are immediately undercut by cheap foreign competition and the industrialist who gives higher wages is put out of business. So Conservatism contents itself with a quiet drift to disaster in the hope that endless repetition of the the prosperity may by medieval incantation invoke prosperity. Labour, on the other hand, turns to remedies which make confusion worse confounded on the lines pursued by Mr. Leon Blum, the Jewish Socialist Prime Minister of France, who was hailed by Mr. Attlee as a model for the Labour Party just before he fell from power, leaving French economics in chaos. Because it is impossible for Labour genuinely to increase purchasing power in face of the sweated competition of the international system, which they support, they turn to the false creation of illusory purchasing power by the disastrous measure of inflation.

This process was well described in the City columns of Labour's organ, the "*Daily Herald*," in an eulogy of their other foreign hero, Mr. Roosevelt. "In modem conditions a reforming Government must maintain a constant stimulus of Government spending ... we have learnt, not that a reforming Government cannot make a system of partly private enterprise work, but that it cannot make it work today without a constantly inflationary pressure . . . The mere pressure of unemployment and of falling Federal revenues will force a big budget deficit on the President."

So the once Socialist Party places its only hope in reformist doctrines which rest on the simple disaster of unbalanced budgets and inflation. This is the Nemesis of making great promises within the limits of a system that cannot deliver the goods. This is the fatality of supporting international Socialism in an age when only National Socialism can work. To inflate means to increase the supply of money without any corresponding increase in the supply of goods, and the result is on historic record in all countries that have tried it. Prices rising far more rapidly than wages diminish the real wages of the workers and create a speculators' paradise, with vast profits for the Stock Exchanges and rising cost of food and living to the people. Inflation and the opposite policy of deflation, which was pursued by the previous Labour Government, alike serve none but the financier who lives by flux and chaos. Inflation with a continually rising price level diminishes real wages and makes speculators' profits. Deflation by continually depressing the price level throws thousands into unemployment and increases the burden of all dead weight debt by making the fixed interest of the bond holder more valuable than it was before.

Each process serves the financiers alone; the first process was the policy of the last Labour Government and the second process would be the policy of the next. For Labour is prevented by an obsolete international creed from pursuing the only solution of building high British wages within a British economic system to enable the British people to consume what the British people produce. Any fool can inflate and appropriately enough this is the only remedy now left to the Labour Party.

They talk of "public works" and certainly public works of a useful and remunerative character should be undertaken by any vigorous Government to bridge the gulf between the breakdown of the present economic system and the creation of a new. The writer, when a Minister in the last Labour Government, planned such works with such an object on a great scale and pressed them without avail on that Government to the point of resignation. But public works undertaken in perpetuity without any serious intention of building a new economic system can have only one result. They pile up the burden of public debt which has to be supported from the declining revenue of a decaying system. This artificial attempt to supply a substitute for the purchasing power of the people in the end makes disaster worse, if indefinitely pursued as an alternative to the building of a new economic system. Public works, therefore, are only justified to bridge the gulf between the old and the new systems.

The Obsolescence of International Socialism

That Labour now has no serious intention of even attempting the building of a new system is all too clear. They are paralysed into ineffective and ever disastrous reformist doctrines by new and modern facts which their original theorists could not foresee, and the present leaders of Labour are incapable of fresh original thought.

The new facts which have destroyed the theory of international Socialism and in practice reduced it to an ineffective and disastrous reformism are plain to see. The first fact is the sweating of Eastern labour by Western finance to undercut the standards of the West. This event has already been examined and alone renders impossible international Socialism. The second fact is that international Socialism has always rested on the theory summarised in the slogan "workers of the world unite," and that after 80 years of this appeal the workers of the world are further than ever from unity. On the contrary, in the interval capitalism has got on with the task of introducing new and sweated workers who are incapable even of reading a Socialist manifesto. Therefore, all hope of freeing themselves from the consequences of internationalism by effective international action has completely faded. The third fact is that the evolutionary method of the Labour Party has become entirely unsuited to an age of revolutionary fact. In practice revolution by the method of evolution has proved a contradiction in terms. Facts move too fast for the Labour Party and the process of nationalising one or two industries and awaiting results before taking "the next step" becomes a farcical delusion in a period during which the whole economic system threatens to collapse about our ears.

While an economic system crashes the only contribution of Labour's evolutionary method is to nationalise one or two of the most obsolete industries, of course, with full compensation, as they always emphasise, to the dispossessed capitalist. So Labour is left holding the baby of decaying industry while the rogues of capitalism make merry with the proceeds of "compensation" in the decadence of a dying system, and the arms of Government are cluttered with their discarded and exhausted offspring. The "inevitability of gradualness" and nationalisation step by step with the hope of arriving at the Socialist State in the course of several generations have become doctrines too absurd to be tenable in the face of the modern electorate. So, at a loss for any effective plans of universal action which can only rest on the principle of power in Government, that in principle Labour denies, they tamely accept their Trade Union Leaders complete negation of Socialism which was summarised by Mr. Bevin's remarkable statement: "We must consider carefully the question how far the State should be permitted to interfere in the regulation of wages and conditions.

Our Movement is a voluntary one, and the claim for State regulation must not be carried too far. It might easily lead us on to the slippery slope of the totalitarian state" (Trade Union Congress, reported in the *Manchester Guardian*, 7/9/37). Their original theory thus entirely abandoned, Labour falls back in practice on the "reformist" doctrines of inflation after the model of Blum and Roosevelt. In so doing Labour performs its classic role and fulfils its historic destiny. For international Socialism is one of the chief instruments of chaos by which lives international finance.

In every sphere of national and world policy we find today international Socialism and international finance marching hand in hand. International Socialism creates, by weakness in Government and muddled folly in method, the flux and the chaos on which battens and thrives the financial parasite of the world.

Finance and Flux

By flux lives the financier and by flux dies the producer. The financier in the inner ring buys at the bottom and sells out at the top. To him, therefore, it is essential that a bottom and top should exist, or in other words that flux should exist. The producer, however, before all else requires stability. To him the greatest disaster is that the price level should be lower when he sells his goods than when he produces his goods. Yet this occurs in every depression of the system of flux by which the financier lives.

The up and down of the economic system, in what are called booms and depressions, are poison to industry but the life blood of finance. Such fluctuation provides the normal business of finance, but in recent years greater and richer harvests have come its way in the sudden crash of currencies and economic systems. Before the pound was devalued in 1931 and the franc in 1937 it was a happy coincidence for the financiers that the respective Socialist Prime Ministers in Britain and France (old "model" MacDonald and new "model" Blum) should assure their nations that never, in any circumstances, would pound or franc be devalued. The interval during which the currencies were sustained by public belief in these statements enabled the financiers to get their money out of the country at a high rate of exchange, and later after devaluation to make enormous profits by bringing it back at a low rate of exchange.

Further fortune fell to the financiers towards the close of 1937, when the prosperity boosting of Conservative ministers gave such confidence to small investors that stock markets for the time held up fairly well, no doubt with the result that big financiers were able to unload on the public in a good market with a view later to buying back when prices touched bottom. But these are rare and refreshing prizes of finance apart from the normal business of profiting by the flux of the system.

Gambling in Commodities

To understand the present fate of the producer it is necessary to study how the flux of the international system is created. The flux of the system arises from the unlimited mobility of inter optional finance and the unlimited power to gamble in the primary commodities which supply the productive industries of the world. It is notable that each post war depression has been preceded by a large rise in the price of primary commodities, followed by a collapse in price. This is due for the most part to gambling by financiers in the raw materials that supply the industries of the world. The immense power of modern production responds immediately to boom demand by an increase in production which exceeds even boom demand. Glut is the result because even a boom of the present system is inadequate to absorb production by reason of the fact that the ultimate market of the people's purchasing power is insufficient. Therefore, glut arises in relation to effective demand and price collapse ensues, with all the familiar phenomena of depression. Finance greatly accentuates the chronic tendency to overproduction, born of under-consumption, by speculation, particularly in primary products, directly a boom increase in demand sets in motion a tendency to increasing price.

So the natural tendency of a system which lacks fundamental purchasing power, for reasons already examined, to produce glut and price collapse, is accentuated to the point of disaster by financial speculation which preys upon the deep-rooted disease of the system. The quick jumping financier is in on the rising market and out of the falling market with a fat profit, while the producers of the world are left to hold the baby in a market of falling prices. It is true that in longer and slower swing of the pendulum between boom and depression these factors would in any case arise in an international system which is inherently incapable of balancing the power of production by consumption. But the increasing and violent oscillations of the system, which today approaches collapse, are due to the financial parasite fastening on to the weak point of the international system and, like a microbe of disease, gravely aggravating a congenital weakness. Internationalism might muddle along a few years more albeit with great suffering to the mass of the people, but the financial microbe of decadence produces a fever which may before long prove fatal. By fever the financier lives but the body of industry perishes.

Wall Street Dictatorship

The same power of almost unlimited mobility of finance in practice subordinates completely the economy of Britain to the economy, or rather chaos, of a foreign country. Finance in the City of London is so interlocked with finance in Wall Street, New York, that in practice the City of London has become a sub-branch of Wall Street. Let anyone who doubts this study the immediate reaction on the London Stock Exchange of any movement on Wall Street. For London follows Wall Street entirely irrespective of British conditions. In recent years adverse movements on the London Stock Exchange have followed adverse movements on Wall Street even in face of good British trade reports. On the other hand, upward movements on the London Stock Exchange have followed an upswing on Wall Street, even in face of a disastrous British unemployment return the previous day. What matters to finance in the City of London is not what is happening in British industry, but what is happening in Wall Street, New York.

Therefore, as under the present system the City of London controls British industry, the life of this nation in the final analysis is controlled by a sub-branch of Wall Street finance. A British farmer may be deprived of his livelihood because a gamble in the Chicago Wheat Pit has produced a collapse in price. A prosperous British industry may suddenly be reduced to a standstill because Wall Street speculation in primary commodities has brought a subsequent fall on the Wall Street Stock Exchange with consequent fall in the City of London, and a downward swing of all prices into depression. Thousands of Britons may walk the streets in unemployment because some big rogue of finance on the other side of the world has gambled in the raw materials of industry.

In fact, the British craftsman will make less money by studying and perfecting his craft than by studying the symptoms of Wall Street. Ironic indeed is the tragedy of this dependence for a people which possesses within our own great heritage of Empire the means to produce every raw material and every commodity we require, not only in abundance but in complete independence of world supply or world speculation.

Finance Power Over Government

This same power of almost unlimited mobility which the international system confers upon finance affords it also almost unlimited power over Governments which support the international system. It is inherent in the system that capital and credit shall have power of movement from one country to another. The power of the financier as an individual to shift his fortune in and out of the country is entirely unrestricted. If these great mobile forces of finance are suddenly transferred from one country to another the exchange of the deserted country begins to collapse and financial panic ensues, which in turn is followed by the collapse of government. The mere threat of this manoeuvre broke the weak Labour Government in 1931, and the execution of this tactic immediately broke Leon Blum's Socialist Government in France shortly after it had been hailed as a "model" by the leader of the British Labour Party. Yet despite this experience the Labour Party dare not include in its programme even a reference to a restriction on the right of the great financiers to wield a power which at any time can break a Labour Government or any other Government. The reason is that the international system, which the Labour Party supports, is innately dependent on international finance. It relies on the financier to supply credit for the international transit and sale of goods and capital for the "promotion of export trade" by foreign loans. The supply of these facilities by the great finance houses makes utterly dependent upon them the whole system of international trade, and in turn renders dependent upon them any Government which supports that system of trade. The reason, therefore, is not far to see why no mention of the great finance houses of the City of London has ever appeared in any programme of the Labour Party. So far from proposing to restrict their masters, like the primitive savage they hold it impious even to mention the name of their God. Labour's financial proposals are confined to the meaningless gesture of nationalising the Bank of England, which for all practical purposes under any strong system of Government is nationalised already.

In simple fact the power of international finance is absolute over all the old parties, because the operation of the system which they support gives finance at any time the power to break them.

Foreign Lending - the Disaster of the System

When we analyse the power of finance over the old parties it is not difficult to see why a system is maintained which serves the financier alone, although it is destructive in modern conditions of every producer's interest, and is disastrous not only to the economy but to the integrity of the nation. Finance is the master of the parties, and finance forbids the building of a national system to meet modern facts and maintains an international system whose obsolescence provides the parasite of decadence with profit. Not only is that profit provided by speculation in the fever of the system which has already been examined. The traditional business of finance under the present system depends on the maintenance of internationalism and is admittedly brought to an end by the creation of an Empire system. That traditional business is foreign lending which we have earlier observed has equipped against us our foreign competitors all over the world, and in recent years has exploited the East to the threatened ruin of the West.

The only motive of foreign lending is to derive a higher rate of interest from the equipment of our competitors than from the equipment of British industry. That interest can only be drawn annually from foreign nations in the shape of gold, services, or goods. As few of them have either gold or services to offer the annual interest on foreign loans is derived almost entirely from the import of foreign goods. Consequently the business of finance depends on foreign imports, because without such imports it cannot draw usury from abroad. Therefore, the interest of finance conflicts directly with the interest of the producer, because imports from abroad are a necessity to finance but a disaster to the producer For it should further be noted that the entry of foreign goods representing interest on foreign loans is not balanced by any corresponding exports of British goods. They are tribute from one country to another in respect of a past transaction without any countervailing payment. In fact their economic effect is precisely the same as the payment of German reparations after the war, which represented tribute from one country to another, in respect of the past transaction of the war, without any balancing export. The effect on the economy of the recipient was then clearly observed and denounced by the international parties of the Left, who now affect to regard interest payments on foreign loans as an unmixed blessing. International Socialism had no use for foreign tribute which entered the national exchequer, but has every use for foreign tribute which enters the private pocket of high finance. The economic effect of either transaction is equally disastrous to British economy, but the Labour Party draws a distinction in favour of the private interest, which is one of the many curious paradoxes of contemporary politics.

Thus the part of international lending in our national economy is clear. It is firstly to supply backward nations with the means to undercut us in the markets of the world, and secondly to draw a high rate of usury from the transaction in the shape of cheap sweated goods, which enter the British market to the complete displacement of British labour because they are balanced by no form of export. Yet the extension of foreign lending has been laid before the country as the highest ambition of British industry in almost all Mr. Neville Chamberlain's annual orations to the Bankers' Dinner as Chancellor of the Exchequer, while the theory of foreign lending and the rights of foreign investors are eagerly championed by the Labour Party.

Behind this theory every influence of the Press and old world economists is also arrayed. British Union challenges, root and branch, the whole conception of foreign lending. We have already observed that the result is interest payment in the shape of foreign goods, which displaces British labour by sweated labour as surely as if thousands of Japanese were imported to Lancashire and Yorkshire to take British jobs. We will now examine the original effect of a foreign loan which means the permanent divorce of British wealth from British consumers for the benefit, or rather for the exploitation, of foreign countries. That wealth, as a capital sum, can never return to this country, for the repayment of the capital of all foreign loans in the shape of foreign goods would not merely disrupt industry like the payment of interest, but would completely shatter the British economic system. So foreign loans mean in practice the permanent consumption of British produced wealth by foreigners and the permanent loss of that wealth to the Britons who produced it.

Yet the whole conspiracy of politicians, Press and economists teaches the British people to believe that to send steel to a remote country to build a bridge over a far away river, and to send bicycles for savages to ride over the bridge, without any hope of repayment of this exported wealth, is a transaction of sound economy and finance. While to keep that steel at home to build British dwellings, and the bicycles at home for Britons to ride along well made roads, is a principle of wild cat finance. The greatest of all bluffs put over the British people is the loan-export bluff, for it has induced them to alienate from themselves forever an enormous proportion of the wealth they have produced by the genius of their technicians and the sweat of their workers. Late in the day they begin to see that the export of machines which they created, and taught the world to use, is today resulting in the equipment of sweated labour to undercut them on every market in the world. Finance, secure in the equipment of the East by the effort of the West, cynically deserts the origin of its strength and wealth for fresh Oriental pastures, where the yield of usury from the sweated is greater than the return of interest from the civilised. So in the final frenzy of the system finance drives the West to produce the means of its own destruction, and, not content even with this classic business of the money power, our financial masters now make the primary commodities and raw materials which serve our stricken industries the subject of world gambles whose fluctuations create a chaos in which industry is prostrated. But internationalism and the parasite which drives it to destruction have gone too far; and today greed and folly bring their Nemesis in the threatened destruction of the body on which they prey. That body is the industry and life of Western Man.

British Union Economic System

BRITISH Union recognises the disintegration of the system and will not attempt to reform the system. The machine in modern conditions has broken and a new machine is required to meet modern fact. By this we do not mean that we shall ever destroy for the sake of destroying or uproot existing institutions merely because they now exist. That was the fallacy of international Socialism, which began with the theory of changing everything and ended with the practice of changing nothing. On the contrary, whatever is good we shall preserve and adapt to a new synthesis and harmony of the nation, while ruthlessly cutting away the dead wood of obsolescence and decadence. The essence of our economic creed is the realist facing of facts and the adoption, even more in practice than in theory, of the quickest means of securing the essentials of national reconstruction. To that end we seek to reconcile every motive of individual exertion with the welfare of the nation as a whole.

The interest of the nation transcends the interest of every faction, but, in recognising the over-riding interest of the community, the individual as a member of the nation secures his own ultimate advantage. Every great institution of our national and traditional life which is workable and can be adapted to new ends will be preserved and woven into a new national pattern and purpose.

Empire System

Above all, we are determined not wantonly to discard but to turn to high advantage the heritage won for our generation by the heroism and sacrifice of those who have gone before. The conjunction of the vast resources of our Empire with the genius of modern science can solve the problem of our age. We are no weak nation stripped of overseas possessions and denied access to raw materials, for our past has bequeathed as opportunity to the present one quarter of the surface of the globe. Therefore, in pride of our past and in confidence of our present abilities we turn to the Empire as the basis of our economic system. In so doing we ask what other alternative is open to our generation? what other means have we either of finding an outlet for our production in face of closing world markets, or of winning freedom from finance tyranny which rules through the obsolescence and decadence of the international system?

If we believe from the evidence of our eyes and of every present experience that internationalism is outworn and in continuance threatens the very life of our industrial system and national integrity, what alternative to that system can we discover except an Empire alternative? If the analysis of the last chapter be accepted, or even in part accepted we are driven to our own Empire as the only alternative to chaos and exploitation.

The only relevant question to the modern mind is whether or not the Empire can supply the modern alternative to the breakdown of the obsolete international system. Can an Empire system afford to our people not merely as good a material life as they possess today, but a higher standard of civilisation than the world has yet seen? To that question we return an unhesitating "yes," and prelude a detailed description of the system with the statement of certain facts which none has yet been found to deny.

1. Within these islands and the Empire are workers whose skill is second to none in the world.

2. Within these islands and the Empire we possess technicians and can produce machinery second to none in the world.

3. Within the Empire alone we possess practically every resource of raw material which industry can possibly require.

4. Within the Empire alone and with our own resources of men, machines, and raw materials, we can immensely increase our present wealth production, provided we have a market for which to produce.

These facts have not yet been challenged and, unless they can be disproved, it is possible to build in our Empire alone, without the need of any assistance from the outside world of chaos, a far higher standard of life than we possess today or than mankind has yet witnessed. But all depends on the condition of the last proposition stated above. Empire industry must have a market for which to produce and that is nothing else but the power of our people to consume. We have studied in the last chapter the factors which deprive the British people of the ability to consume the goods which they produce. Deliberately we build an Empire system that rests on the simple principle that the British people shall consume what the British people produce.

Home Market

The first act in the building of a new system is clearly to free the people of these islands from the forces which deprive them of purchasing power and to build a home market which rests on the high purchasing power of the people. High wages is a basic principle of our economic system, because high wages alone can give the people the power to consume the goods which they produce. The first factor which prevents high wages at present is the undercutting of British labour, even on the home market, by cheap foreign products often far below in price our present production costs.

To this situation we apply the simple principle that nothing shall be imported into Britain which can be produced within Great Britain. The implementing of this principle means the exclusion from these islands of some £360 millions of manufactured and agricultural products which are now imported annually. To replace these by British products, on any current computation of production and employment, will give employment to nearly a million and a half of our people. In addition, British industry will be free on the home market from the cheap foreign competition which today holds down wages and diminishes the extent and purchasing power of the home market.

But British Union system for the home market does not end there for it would be idle to prevent the undercutting of British labour by sweated goods from abroad if we still permitted the undercutting of British labour by sweated goods produced at home. It is useless to protect our standard of life from the foreign employer who pays low wages if we still expose it to the attack of the British employer who pays low wages. To meet this situation British Union constitutes the Corporate system, and the effect of that system in preventing sweated production within Great Britain is plain and direct.

The first objective of the great industrial Corporations will be the elimination of sweated competition from within, when the Government, by exclusion, has eliminated sweated competition from without. They will lay down the minimum wage rate over the sphere of industry which they cover and infringement of these wage rates will be a criminal offence. But the function of the Corporations will be not merely static but dynamic. It will be their task progressively to adjust consumption to production power, and thus to overcome for the benefit of industry and people the problems created by rationalisation and our ever advancing industrial and mechanical technique. In other words, it will be the duty of the Corporations to raise wages and salaries over the whole sphere of industry as science and industrial technique increase the power to produce. Consequent on the elimination of sweated competition, both from without and from within, no limit will exist to the extent to which producing power can thus be increased except the limit set by scientific and productive advance.

When the purchasing power of our own people is so high that their demand provides a market for the labour of every man and woman who wants a job, and for the full capacity of every machine, we must call a halt until further scientific achievement makes possible a further advance in the standard of life. For to increase purchasing power without a corresponding increase in the production of goods is to incur the disaster of inflation. On the other hand, an increase of purchasing power, accompanied by a planned advance in the production of goods, is not inflation but an increase in the production and consumption of real wealth. Thus we shall arrive at the point of true civilisation, when useful employment can be found for the whole population and for all machinery, and the main question of that future will be whether further to increase production or to reduce the hours of labour. For the final solution of the present problem which is miscalled "overproduction" is both to increase wages and to reduce the hours of labour, thus at last making man the master of machine instead of the machine the master of man.

Position of Individual Firms - Tory Protection

We seek to build a home market in which the British can consume what the British produce by the joint method of excluding sweated products from without and the prohibition of sweated production from within. The relative position of individual firms will remain the same on the new high wage basis as on the present low wage basis. If you compel A to raise wages but permit his rival B to maintain low wages the only effect is to put A out of business by giving an advantage to his rival B. But if you compel both A and B to raise wages their relative competitive position remains the same. Under British Union system any individual is free to put his rival out of business by greater efficiency than his rival, but he is not free to put his rival out of business by paying lower wages. The essential difference between the economic "insulation" of British Union policy and any protective proposals ever advanced by the Conservative Party can thus easily be discerned. We will assume, for the sake of argument, that the incredible happened and that the Conservative Party gave to industry the real protection from foreign competition which they have always promised at elections, in glaring contradiction of their practice when they recently possessed record majorities in Government and yet permitted the annual import into these islands of £360 millions of foreign manufactures and agricultural products. If the miracle occurred and Conservative pledges were actually carried out this vital difference would exist between their policy even in this regard and that of British Union. Behind their protective barrier no organisation would exist to prevent the production of sweated goods and unfair undercutting by low wages of one British firm by another.

Conservative rejection of the Corporate system deprives them of any means to this end. Consequently, despite their protection, British wages would still be kept down by sweated competition from within even if they had eliminated sweated competition from without. A further evil undoubtedly would arise under this unregulated and anarchic system which provides freedom only for the exploiter to exploit. Freed from all check and threat of foreign competition under Conservative protection the present tendency towards trust, combine and monopoly would greatly accelerate. Even more combines would come together to exploit the protected market without any let or hindrance. The classic tendency of the monopoly would quickly emerge in the increase of price to the consumer and the decrease of wage to the worker. Consequently protection unaccompanied by organisation and power in Government is an unmitigated evil. On the other hand, insulation from world chaos is the first and necessary action in the building of an economic system which can only thrive and advance in the high purchasing power of the mass of the people.

Imports, Exports and Empire

Thus British Union builds a home market capable of absorbing the maximum production of British industry, subject only to the necessity of acquiring outside these islands what we cannot here produce. At this point we turn to our own Empire overseas to secure the raw materials and some foodstuffs which Great Britain cannot produce. We shall offer to our Dominions and Colonies the direct bargain for which they have always asked. We will buy from them raw materials and any foodstuffs which we cannot produce here on condition that they accept an equivalent value of our manufactures in return. They are primarily producers of raw materials and foodstuffs and we are now primarily producers of manufactures and exports such as coal. A natural balance of Empire economy exists which policy in this country has done much to destroy by preferring to buy essential raw materials and food from foreign countries. As a result the Dominions have already been driven to the development of secondary manufacturing industries. That process, if long continued, may develop in the Dominions an economic self-sufficiency which may lead in time to their complete inability to accept our exports. Great Britain will then be faced with the retribution of internationalism in dependence on foreign supply, for which she can only pay by exporting goods to foreign markets that are rapidly closing against her. In fact, continuance in the policy of preferring the foreign to the Empire supply of raw materials and certain foodstuffs might finally spell the doom of these crowded islands when, in the future, they seek outside supplies for which they cannot make payment either in foreign or Empire markets.

On the other hand, an early development of Empire economic system can arrest the drift to this catastrophe. The process of developing secondary industries in Dominions and Colonies has not yet gone far enough to prevent a balanced Imperial economy. They offer to us still the simple bargain of their raw materials to be balanced by their acceptance of our manufactured exports in a £1 to £1 equivalent.

Why are the international parties, Conservative and Labour alike, so mad as to refuse? The answer to this riddle may be found in the deliberate maintenance of the adverse balance of payments under the existing foreign trade pacts, which should provide a conclusive argument for the abrogation of these pacts in favour of a balanced Empire trade. Under almost every foreign trade pact Britain imports more than she exports in return. The adverse balance of goods received represents interest payments made on past loans without any balancing export in return as described in the last chapter. So Great Britain refuses Empire trade and maintains the adverse balance of trade pacts with foreign nations for the sole reason that the process is a means of collecting the usury of the City of London.

An Empire system is sacrificed and we drift towards the disaster of dependence on an ultimate world system, in which we can find no means of payment for necessary imports, solely because the British Government and our economic system are debt collectors for the City of London. Not only must British labour be displaced in the home market by the import of sweated goods as interest payment, but we are forbidden to develop our heritage in an Empire economy because the millstone of foreign lending is still around our necks. We have to choose between an insulated Empire system, containing within its free boundaries the highest standard of civilisation that the world has yet seen, and the maintenance of a world usury system which in every sphere destroys the productive interest and oppresses the people. We have to choose between Empire and Usury; British Union chooses Empire.

Empire Development

It is clear that our system depends on the intensive development of an Empire which is today producing only a fraction of what it could produce. The question is sometimes asked whether we can rely on the co-operation of the self-governing Dominions with whose self-governing status we have no desire in any way to interfere. The question does not arise in the case of the Crown Colonies, because their control changes with the Government of Britain. In the case of the Dominions it surely follows that they will co-operate in the policy for which they have always asked. It is they who have demanded a market for their raw materials and for such foodstuffs as we could not produce in this country, and it is the Government of Britain who have refused in order to accept goods from foreign countries for reasons above stated. It is inconceivable, therefore, that the Dominions for any political reason should refuse a policy for which they have always asked and that offers to them such an advantage. If any Dominion Government for any purpose of political spite adopted such a course we would rely with complete confidence on the Dominion producer at an early election to sweep them from power, for he would not tolerate the sacrifice of his economic interests to any political prejudice. Our appeal for Dominion cooperation is based not only on kinship and history, but on an overriding mutual economic interest.

In the case of the Crown Colonies we affirm frankly that what has been won by the heroism of the British people shall be used for the benefit of the British people. Instruments like the Congo Basin Treaty, which are supported by the Conservative Party and make our African possessions the dumping ground of the world, will be repudiated, and British possessions will be preserved as a British market, with a result in itself, that current statistics prove, will go far to restoring our export trade. The great British colonial tradition of good and fair treatment of native populations will be preserved, but we shall challenge the illusion that backward and illiterate populations are fit for self-government when obviously they are not. Nor do we admit that the Western nations should be confronted with closed areas in the supposed interests of native populations, which have done nothing to develop their own territory before the genius of the Western mind and energy put them on the map of the world.

If "Left" theories in this sphere were logically applied America would be handed back to the original Red Indian inhabitants, and the white man would be barred from the land which his talent has created. In practice these high-sounding theories of native self-determination have resulted in no higher reality than the ruthless sweating and exploitation of native populations by Western finance capitalists for the undercutting of the Western standard of life. In practice native "rights" have been the right to be exploited. Such exploitation of backward populations will be absolutely forbidden in British Union Empire, and as a result the poison stream of sweated goods will no longer enter the arteries from within the body of Empire. Good and fair treatment of native populations is a British tradition, but to stultify the white man's genius in order to preserve native "rights" to neglect fertile areas of the globe, or native "rights" to be exploited by finance capitalists for the destruction of the West, is an historic absurdity and a British tragedy. Therefore, consciously and determinedly we develop for the benefit of the British people the territory which the energy of the British people has made their own.

Agriculture

In developing the territory of our Empire British Union policy by no means forgets the development of our own native soil. The measures already described will not only save agriculture, but are the only measures that can save British agriculture. For our policy meets the two factors which today destroy agriculture and depopulate our countryside. They are (1) the flood of foreign imports, (2) the low purchasing power of our British people which deprives them of the ability to buy good British food.

By present conditions a conflict has been created between town and country in which the countryside has always been worsted since the Conservative Party ceased to be the party of the land and became instead the party of high finance. The farmer must have a better price in order to live and to pay his farm workers the decent wages that he would like to pay if prices permitted. Financial democracy meets his demand with the fact that under the present system the town workers, who are the bulk of the population, are too poor to pay a better price. So agriculture perishes, and the people are uprooted from the soil, with results to whose fatality all history bears witness. British Union policy resolves the conflict between town and country and welds their interests in a new national harmony. Every attempt to solve the agricultural problem in isolation from the national problem as a whole has failed, and will always fail.

British Union overcomes the dilemma of the countryside : (1) By raising the purchasing power of the mass of the people to the point that modern science permits by means already described; (2) By prohibiting entirely the import into Britain of any foodstuffs that can be produced within Great Britain. This policy preserves for British agriculture the home market and provides a market capable of paying for British products. In practice no substantial increase of price to the consumer need be anticipated, and in any event, the general increase in wages and conditions under a modern system will be far greater than any increase in farming prices. The farmer can increase production for an assured market without any very great increase of his present overhead charges. Consequently an increase in production without a commensurate increase in production costs will tend to prevent prices from rising. Yet greater production for an assured market will afford the farmer profit instead of loss, and the labourer a living in place of a starvation wage. In addition a Distributive Corporation will cut our redundant distribution costs and bring farmer and consumer closer together in the absence of a host of unnecessary middlemen who now take their toll of farmer and consumer alike. Measures to prevent profiteering in food are overdue, and if necessary, will be severe. But the basic guarantee of prosperity to British agriculture is the high purchasing power of the British people and that great home market is the constant aim of British Union policy. A market that is capable of paying for British food products can easily be preserved for British agriculture, because if the townsmen can pay for British food they will always prefer it as they know it to be the best.

More British Food

So British Union policy deliberately excludes from these islands all foodstuffs that can be produced within them. This will entail the production of another £200 million of British foodstuffs each year to replace foreign imports that will be excluded. The writer, in addressing hundreds of farmers' meetings throughout the land, has never yet found a farmer to deny that it is possible, provided they have an assured market for which to produce. Clearly it will take some years to evoke the maximum of British production.

In practical method Government will meet the Farmers' Union, which will have an even greater status within the Corporate State, and will inquire by how much British production can be increased in each succeeding year. Government will then undertake to cut down foreign imports by a corresponding amount until, at the end of a specified period, British production has entirely taken the place of the foreign import. The end will then be secured of a market for the full production of British agriculture which rests on the high purchasing power of the British people.

It is true that we cannot here produce all the diverse kinds of foodstuffs that we require. But like our raw materials we can acquire all the outside foodstuffs we need from our own Dominions and Colonies. In a choice between British and Dominion products the British must always come first, but plenty of room will still exist on British markets for Dominion foodstuffs. We now import annually £180 million worth of foodstuffs from the Dominions, and it is possible to increase British production by £200 million a year at the expense of the foreigner alone, without touching Dominion imports. Further, any cut in any particular branch of Dominion imports which it is necessary to make in the interests of British farming will be far more than compensated by the much greater demand of the British people for other Dominion and Colonial products, and raw materials, when our purchasing power is increased. British and Dominion production will divide between them a greatly increased British market on the principle of Britain First, Dominions and Colonies second, and the foreigner nowhere.

Foreign Food Prices

The absence of the foreign food product from the British market is a distressing thought to those international parties, Conservative and Labour alike, who have taught the people that to buy abroad is to buy cheap. But the people are no longer impressed, for they have found in fact that to buy abroad is to buy dear. In all recent sudden rises in food prices the rise in price of the foreign has greatly exceeded the rise in price of the British product. The reason is that the combine and monopoly have invaded also the control of the people's food. Immediately a tendency to price rise occurs the foreign monopolies rush up the price of food to the British consumer. If the international parties were allowed to carry the financier's game much further, and the British consumer by the ruin of British farming became completely at the mercy of foreign supply, the British people would find that to buy abroad from the foreign food combines was the dearest folly that they had ever committed.

The import of foreign foodstuffs is pursued as a sacred rite of the financial democratic system because those imports more than any other pay the interest on foreign loans as previously described. But as ever in decadence parasite grows on parasite, and today the policy of foreign food combines is to undercut and put the British farmer out of business in order that they may have the British consumer completely at their mercy. This crime has been permitted and encouraged by Conservative Governments which have given to the British farmer the "Board" and to the foreign combine the "Market."

Organisation for a market which does not exist is in any case without purpose. The old parties have merely given to the farmer restriction when all he needed was opportunity. The British farmer may be trusted to carry on his own business once he has a market for which to produce. He must be freed from the foreign import which destroys him, and the redundant middleman who exploits him, to serve a market which is capable of paying him a living. This Government can do this for farming and more, for every method of modern science and organisation to help the farmer in his task must be made available to British agriculture. British Union knows that no people can live that is uprooted from the soil and that the universal urbanisation of a population spells a doom inevitable and historic. British Union knows too that the men who carried British genius and the glory of our name and our achievement to the far corners of the earth, had roots deep in the soil of our native land. The little men and the little parties in the service of an alien finance have tried to sever the roots of the oak. We who come from the soil of Britain say that the oak shall stand.

The People's State - A Classless System

Heredity

THE system of British Union provides no place for the parasite. It has neither privilege nor place for those who seek to live on the efforts of others without giving anything in return. But the people's state has opportunity and place for all who serve the nation in an infinite variety of capacity. So British Union system of heredity is accordingly designed on the one hand to encourage to the utmost the initiative and enterprise of the individual not only in working for himself but also in deep and human motive in working for his children. On the other hand, it is devised to eliminate the parasite and to deprive of all hereditary advantage those who prove unworthy of their forebears' exertions and unworthy of the new nation. Therefore, a man, or woman, may by energy and enterprise not only enrich themselves but bequeath the result of their efforts to their children. But the children, either in industrial service or in public service, must render a service equivalent to the benefit they receive, or in default will lose their hereditary advantage in whole or in part. Equity Tribunals of People's Justice will be established to determine on commonsense lines such questions, which will be no more difficult to settle than many questions of equity that come before the courts today. The system will be woven quite naturally and easily into a general codification and simplification of the law of the land, in language which anyone can understand without dependence on a lawyer's racket.

The Land

Opportunities for public service on a far greater scale than exists today will be provided by the immense development in the social life of the new nation, which will call for leadership and effort in many spheres now closed. For one example, a real local leadership will again be required in a revitalised countryside. The original owners of the land in most cases gave such leadership until death duties and the victory of urbanism broke the system. They will again have such opportunity in British Union system, which seeks consciously the continuity of a stock with roots in the soil, and will accordingly lift from the land death duties and other burdens in return for real service to the land. But the landlord whose time, money, and energy are not spent among his own people in local leadership but are divided between a London night club and a continental resort will be ruthlessly dispossessed without any compensation. The land thus acquired by the State will be used for the development of owner occupier farms, and a mixed system of local leadership and owner occupier will result which will preserve the best traditions of the land and afford the maximum stability.

To the urban landlord British Union applies the same principle as to any other monopolist. Any attempt to exploit a shortage of any commodity by increasing the price to the people will be rigorously suppressed. So all rents will be controlled by law while any shortage of housing exists. As for the slum landlord he will simply be dispossessed without compensation and prosecuted like any other purveyor of commodities which are a danger to health. The landlord who without effort of his own seeks to take advantage of community effort by increasing the price of land in the neighbourhood of an expanding town or industry will be confronted by a simple dilemma. He will be taxed on his own valuation of the land, but the State will have power to acquire it at that valuation. If he assesses the value at a high figure he will be taxed at a high figure, and if he assesses it at a low figure he will be bought out at that figure with increment to the nation. Thus British Union will solve the ancient problem of "land values" by measures which place the land in the same category as any other potential monopoly. In practice, however, most ownership of urban land will pass to the State as that category of landlord is a great deal less likely than the leader of the countryside to justify his hereditary wealth by public service. It is unfair to discriminate between the land and any other form of hereditary wealth, but he who lives on the land without service to the nation will pass with other parasites.

Class

Liberal Socialism has ever striven to represent that only one form of hereditary wealth led to vicious results, namely the land in which their leading figures happened to have no interest. In fact, the worse vices of the hereditary system which British Union will sweep away arise from the transmission of hereditary wealth by quickly rich financiers and speculators, whose children have no sense whatever of hereditary responsibility in return for hereditary wealth. To such as these the "trustee of the nation" principle of all wealth owners under British Union are utterly lacking. From them, in particular, has come the disgusting spectacle of flaunting extravagance and paraded riches in face of poverty, which evoked from British Union the principle that "none shall stuff while others starve." Above all they have created the fatal distinctions of social class which British Union is determined to remove for ever. Their class values are based on money value and on nothing else. The accident of birth and the mere fact of being their "father's son" is held by these miserable specimens of modern degeneracy to elevate them without effort of their own above their fellow men. Not only are they given opportunity by their forebears's exertion, but many of them neglect that opportunity for any other end than the idle pursuit of pleasure, while they cumber the directorates of their hereditary businesses which underpaid technicians conduct. Here we see the apotheosis of the parasite deriving his snobbery from his father's efforts and marking the values of the snob by the capacity to squander in face of the starving. The snob and the parasite shall go, and with him shall go his values in the classless state which accords "opportunity to all but privilege to none."

Function

Class based on social snobbery and the accident of inheritance shall go. But British Union will not fall into the opposite stupidity of an unworkable equalitarianism which refuses to recognise between man and man or woman and woman any difference of function. A man shall be valued by what he is and not by what his father was. If he performs high service to the nation in the exercise of exceptional capacity he shall have fitting reward and status. To work, not only for money for self and children, but for position and honour among fellow men is no small and unworthy motive of mankind, and is a deep mainspring of human conduct which it is folly to ignore. The award of honour as the reward of money may go to great service and may be transmitted to children, but like hereditary wealth will be liable to removal if the children are unworthy.

To argue that all men are the same and that exceptional effort is worthy of no recognition is an error that robs of motive power important human enterprises. It is true that the great lights of humanity have illumined the path of mankind from no other motive than the inner light. But it is folly to ignore the fact that the overwhelming majority who achieve anything are moved by simple terms of honourable distinction and the winning of security for home and children. It is still greater folly to presume that all men are equally gifted in mind, muscle, or spirit; from that fallacy arises the fatal tendency of the present phase to slow down the pace of the fastest to that of the slowest. This grotesque assumption, if carried to its logical conclusion, would merely deprive the nation of the full exertion of exceptional ability by which alone great affairs can be conducted.

Education

The true solution is to eliminate the parasite of heredity but to give the utmost opportunity to talent wherever it can be found. Whether a man starts in castle or cottage he shall have equal opportunity to rise to the top and to use his talent if he possesses the capacity. This principle involves a complete revision of the present educational system, which largely confines opportunity to the accident of wealth. In the reconstruction of national education it will be also the deliberate aim of British Union finally to eliminate the last trace of class and snobbery.

Preliminary education will afford to all the same sound basis of classless and national education, subject to the right of all parents to secure for their children the religious atmosphere they desire. But later education will differentiate widely, not on the principle of wealth but purely on the principle of talent. At present the children of the rich are normally educated at least until eighteen years of age, altogether irrespective of their capacity for education. The children of the poor, on the other hand, are largely thrust into industry at the age of fourteen, irrespective of talent for the higher education which is denied. It will be the policy of British Union to continue the education of all by varying methods and degree until eighteen years of age. In the present low standard of life to deprive parents of the small wages of children who displace their elders from industry would be a hardship. In the higher standard of life which science will produce within a modern system adults will earn enough to keep the home together without dependence on the wage pittances of children.

Therefore British Union will render it possible to continue education for all until an age when they can be regarded as truly adult and ready to enter industrial life. But from the age of fifteen onwards education will be sharply and progressively differentiated between varying degrees of talent.

All children of outstanding ability will have open to them by progressive selection a straight road from cradle to university. The opportunity open to every child will be the same, and the same path to higher education will be available to all talent. Those on the other hand who cannot benefit beyond a certain point from the absorption of academic knowledge, as a preliminary to the practical in life, will undergo different forms of education and training, and at an earlier age will specialise for some definite avocation. Above all, every child, of whatever talent or capacity, will receive a sound physical and nutritional basis for the struggle of life. The care of the child is the special care of British Union, for British Union will be not only the nation's trustee of today but also of tomorrow. That infinite morrow of British destiny depends on building a nation with physique and morale adequate to the immense duty of British leadership. In that high purpose we guard the child.

True Patriotism

The people's state of British Union thus secures the principle of opportunity for all but privilege to none. Every Briton shall have equal opportunity in the land of his birth, and, therefore, equal possession and love of that land. Thus shall be born the true patriotism which is determination to build a land worthy of a patriot's love. This is something very different from Conservatism's exploitation of that profound emotion to guard the vested interests which possess Britain today. No wonder that so many of the dispossessed reply to the "Tory patriot" that "it is your land, not our land, that you ask us to defend." Britain looks different to the "father's son" arriving at a night club door in a Rolls Royce than to the man of possibly greater capacity and, in the war at least, of greater service, who is shivering in the rain or fog of a country that has used him and discarded him. In British Union our land will look the same to all, for it will afford to all the same opportunity and so will belong to all.

Today patriotism and progress are divided by the parties into opposing camps when, in fact, they should be indissolubly united. Love of country has been exploited by reaction and hatred of country has been exploited by those who masquerade in the clothes of progress. In reality patriotism dies without progress because the continual advance of man alone can build a country worthy of love. On the other hand, progress dies without patriotism because the first object of progress must be the elevation of the native land, and care for every country but their own has robbed the misnamed parties of progress of all appeal to the enthusiasm and effort of their fellow countrymen. We love our country and we love our people, and for that reason we stand both for patriotism and for progress in the union of two great principles which the war of the parties has divided. The National Socialist creed of British Union says to our countrymen "if you love our country you are National, and if you love our people you are Socialist." We ask patriots to join with us in building a country worthy of a patriot's love, in which the class distinction of the snob and the privilege of the parasite shall exist no more. But in place of class and privilege shall arise the brotherhood of the British to give equal opportunity to all in service and possession of their native land.

The Jewish Question

THE Jewish question should receive proper space in relation to national affairs in any book which deals with the modern problem. This question was no concern of our Movement at the outset, but the Jews themselves very quickly made it a concern. We advanced for the consideration of our countrymen the policy which appears in these pages, without raising any racial question or troubling with any faction. Long before we raised the Jewish question in any form, however, that question was forced on our attention.

The evidence for this statement can be ascertained by any one from police court records. For the inquirer will learn that of those convicted for physical attacks on Blackshirts 50 per cent were undeniably Jewish in the six months which preceded the introduction of this question by the British Union in October,

1934. Our organisation had then been in existence two years and we had observed that, in addition to an extraordinary proportion of Jews in the physical assailants of our members (when out numbered), the victimisation of our people by Jewish employers and the pressure of Jewish interests on our supporters was a very distinctive feature of our struggle. This occurrence forced the Jewish question on the attention of many who had paid no more attention to Jews or their particular problem and character than to any other section of the community.

The resultant study revealed a fact not difficult to ascertain, that a remarkable proportion of Jews were engaged in practices which the system we proposed would bring to an end. Throughout the ages Jews have taken a leading part in international usury and all forms of finance and money lending, while smaller exemplars of the method have engaged in such practices as price cutting, the sweating of labour, and other means of livelihood which any ordered and regulated economy must bring to an end. So the reason was not far to seek why we had incurred the bitter and especial enmity of Jewish interests.

Some say that it is a wicked animal that defends itself when attacked, but the response of the Englishman to a blow in the face is traditional. That response was greeted immediately by all the organs which Jewish interests control with a loud clamour of racial persecution. It is well, therefore, to set down exactly what we propose on this question, and the reader may decide for himself whether this policy is persecution or simple justice which is necessary to the integrity of our own nation.

Rights of the State

We do not attack Jews on account of their religion, for our principle is complete religious toleration, and we certainly do not wish to persecute them on account of their race, for we dedicate ourselves to service of an Empire which contains many different races and any suggestion of racial persecution would be detrimental to the Empire we serve. Our quarrel with the Jewish interests is that they have constituted themselves a state within the nation, and have set the interests of their co-racialists at home and abroad above the interest of the British State.

An outstanding example of this conduct is the persistent attempt of many Jewish interests to provoke the world disaster of another war between Britain and Germany, not this time in any British quarrel, but purely in a Jewish quarrel.

None can argue that it is a principle of racial or religious persecution for a State to lay down the principle that its citizens must own first allegiance to the nation of which they are members and not to any faction at home or abroad. That many Jews regard themselves first as members of Jewry and secondly as British citizens is not only a matter of simple observation but of proof from Jewish literature and statement. British Union, therefore, affirms the simple principle that Jews who have placed the interests of Jewry before those of Britain must leave Great Britain. In particular, those who have indulged in practices alien to British character and tradition must leave these shores. Those against whom no such charge rests will not be persecuted, but will be treated as the majority of their people have elected to be treated. They have maintained themselves as foreigners in our midst and as such they will regarded, without the privileges of the British citizenship which to them has been a secondary consideration.

We British have not been in the habit of persecuting foreigners and we shall not in British Union develop that habit. On the contrary, we have a tradition of according good treatment to foreigners who have particularly served this nation and any such Jews have certainly no reason to anticipate any breach of this tradition. But all nations have a right to say that foreigners who have abused their hospitality shall leave the country, and any State has a right to affirm that all citizens shall own allegiance to the nation and not to any external power.

It remains to inquire whether in fact it is fair to regard the Jew as a foreigner. The simple answer is that he comes from the Orient and physically, mentally and spiritually, is more alien to us than any Western nation. If a community of several hundred thousand Frenchmen, Germans, Italians or Russians were dumped in our midst they would create a grave national problem. That problem would be particularly grave if they maintained themselves as a community in our midst, owning spiritual allegiance to their original nation, and indulging in methods and practices altogether alien to British character and temperament. Such an event would create a problem so serious that a solution would have to be found. Yet the Jew is more remote from British character than any German or Frenchman, for they are Westerners and the Jews are Orientals.

The Final Solution

This problem has been raised with increasing pressure in most European countries in the inevitable opportunity presented to Jewish method by the "decline of the West." It has become a European question of first class magnitude in which Britain must offer leadership in accord with British tradition. It is not in accord with British character to keep Jews here in order to bully them - that we will never do. On the contrary, the statesmanship of the future must find a solution of this question on the lines of the Jews again becoming an integral nation.

There are many waste places of the earth possessing great potential fertility, and the collective wisdom of a new Europe should be capable of finding territory where the Jews may escape the curse of no nationality and may again acquire the status and opportunity of nationhood. It is true that Palestine is not available as a home for the Jewish race throughout the world, for the simple reason that it is already the home of the Arabs. Whatever wrongs the Jews are alleged to have suffered will not be righted by the crime of inflicting with violence far greater wrongs on the Arab ally who trusted the word of

Britain in war. The most that the Jews can reasonably hope from Palestine is respect for their holy places and free access to visit them as the pilgrim Arab has access to Mecca. Other territory must and can be found for the solution of the Jewish problem of the world. Is it really persecution of the Jews to suggest that they should again become a nation in suitable territory? If so, it is persecution which has been acclaimed by the prophets and seers of Jewry as the final objective of their race for the last two thousand years. Their leaders have always proclaimed the wish of Jewry to become again a nation. Why is it persecution to say "very well, you shall become again a nation"? It is not persecution unless it be true that every protestation of Jewry in this regard was hypocrisy throughout the ages, and that their real desire was not to reunite their scattered race in national dignity but to become for ever the parasite of humanity.

If, therefore, Jewish declarations be sincere, the effort of European statesmanship to find a solution of this problem by the creation of a Jewish National State should not be resisted by Jewry. The only thing the Jews cannot ask in the name of justice and humanity is that Britain should found for them that state in blood by the slaughter of Arabs and the rape of their homes.

In summary of our policy on this question we affirm the right of every nation to deport any foreigner who has abused its hospitality, and we hold the aim of finding, together with other European nations, a final solution of this vexed question by the creation of a Jewish National State, in full accord with the age-long prayers of the prophets and leaders of the Jewish race. Is this persecution or is it justice?

British Foreign Policy

The International of Finance and Socialism

BRITISH foreign policy should hold two objectives: (1) the maintenance of British interest; (2) the maintenance of world peace. These two objectives do not conflict but coincide. British Unions deep quarrel with the virtually unanimous policy of the old parties is that it has sacrificed both the interests of Britain and of world peace to a political vendetta. Particularly we denounce the pursuit of that feud to the risk of British lives and world catastrophe because it is dictated by subservience to the vile international interests which command the old parties.

In this sphere international finance and international Socialism march openly hand in hand. They are by nature complementary forces of disaster, for the policy of international Socialism creates the flux and chaos by which finance lives and the producer perishes. Still more, in foreign policy their community of aim and of method should be clear to all, together with the reason of their unholy union. Certain countries have at once extirpated the control of international finance and the hopes of international Socialism. No reason exists in British interest to quarrel with these countries and every reason of world peace forbids the quarrel. Yet the feud of international finance and its twin, international Socialism, thrusts the manhood of Britain toward mortal quarrel with these nations.

Germany and Italy, despite a present poverty of natural resources have, at least, broken the control of international finance, and Germany in particular has offended this world power by summary dealing with the Jewish masters of usury. So every force of the money power throughout the world has been mobilised to crush them, and that power does not stop short at payment for its vendetta in British blood. Any study of the Press and propaganda organs controlled by finance power can reach no other conclusion if we ask the simple question, what single interest of Britain or of world peace is served by their clearly deliberate intention to provoke war between Britain and the new countries?

The motive of international Socialists is equally clear in their new clamour for war at any price. International Socialism has always taught the people that any form of national action in independence of world conditions was futile, and that the success of Socialism in Britain depended on the universal adoption of their doctrines throughout the world. Now great countries arise which have uprooted in theory and practice the obsolete doctrines of international Socialism, and consequently bar to the British Labour Party all hope of the universal acceptance of their creed, on which they admit alone the success of their cause can depend. So but one hope of the ultimate triumph of their party remains to the leaders of Labour, and that is the overthrow of these new systems by the force of world war. Lightly the Labour leaders appear to be prepared to purchase their political objective in British blood, and to pursue their political vendetta at the price of every interest of Britain and of world peace.

The party which has been built on cant of pacifism today leads the clamour for war, and the party which ever refused Britain arms to defend herself now supports rearmament, not for the defence of Britain, but for the defence by war of international Socialism. Foremost in the van of the new jingoes is the Socialist conscientious objector of 1914. So is presented an edifying spectacle which naturally makes but scant appeal to the ex-serviceman of the last war. He replies with British Union that we have fought Germany once in a British quarrel and we shall not fight her again either in a Socialist or in a Jewish quarrel.

Perversion of the League

In result every high aspiration of the war generation has been frustrated and perverted. The League of Nations, which was the repository of many fine ideals, like the Holy Alliance of the previous century, has been perverted to perform exactly the opposite purpose to that which it was intended to fulfill. The League was meant to overcome the division of Europe, and to eliminate for ever the fatal system of the balance of power, which divided mankind into opposing and contending camps of highly armed and hostile nations. It has been perverted to be a new and more vicious instrument of that system by which Britain, France and Russia, in the name of the League, can mobilise their remaining satellite powers in one balance of a scale, whose other balance, by force of a common original adversity, now holds the armed power of Germany, Italy and Japan.

Despite every aspiration of the war generation and every hope of stricken mankind we are back where we began in a situation which for Britain is more dangerous than before. For the departure by present Government, in their political vendetta, from the sober British policy of pursuing the coincident objectives of peace and British interests has resulted in follies of which British statesman ship has never previously been guilty. Never before in modern times have we placed ourselves in a strategical position so vulnerable that any child could observe it and also apprehend the consequence. We face Germany across the North Sea and Japan in the far seas of our Eastern possessions, while in the Mediterranean route to our Oriental Empire we have succeeded in antagonising at one end the new Spain, and at the other end the Arabs, with an alienated Italy in the middle. With Germany and the Arabs we have quarreled for the sake of the Jews, and with Italy and the new Spain for the sake of international Socialism in an alliance with Russian Communism. Has British statesmanship ever before perpetrated folly on a scale so gigantic, in denial so complete of British interest, security and peace?

Conservative Alliance with Communism

The virtual alliance of Conservative Government in Britain with Communist Government in Russia is at the root of all evil in foreign policy. This curious communion of Conservatism and Communism in the international sphere will not appear so strange to those familiar at home with British Union struggle, who have witnessed again and again the deliberate use by Conservatism of a Communism which, in myopic vision, they do not fear against the creed of the twentieth century, which has excited both the panic and the fury of reaction. Constantly

Conservatism has condoned, excused, and even supported the crimes of Communism when the target was fellow Britons who dared to raise against Conservative betrayal of the people the standard of a new and true patriotism.

Abroad, as at home, Conservatism is willing to use even the vile and bloody instrument of world Communism against the nations of European renaissance. That a virtual alliance exists between the Government of Britain and that of Moscow, with the natural and warm approval of the Socialist opposition, is not today denied. The Franco Soviet Pact has ever been approved by the Conservative Government and the close association of French and British policy, together with the close cooperation of British and Russian policy at Geneva and elsewhere, has almost flaunted in the face of Europe the triple alliance of Britain, France and Russia, to which the overwhelming majority of the British people are completely opposed.

Arms Race Origin

The full historic error of the Franco Soviet Pact can only be appreciated if the chronology of these events is recalled. In November, 1933, the leader of Germany made an offer to Europe which fell into three parts: (1) limitation of German naval strength in fixed ratio to British strength; (2) limitation of German air force to 50 per cent the strength of France; (3) limitation of German army to 300,000 men if France would agree to the same restriction. This offer is on historic record, and also the answer to that offer; for the reply of France, without any protest from Great Britain, was the Franco-Soviet Pact. Only the naval offer was accepted by Britain, with beneficial results, because German naval strength in the outcome of negotiations was limited to a 85 per cent ratio of British strength, and a fatal recurrence of the pre-war naval race between Britain and Germany was averted. The offer of air and land limitation was contemptuously ignored and answered only with the Franco-Soviet Pact, which Germany regarded as an attempt to encircle her. From that moment the sequence of fatality has been clear. Germany armed in a prodigious effort and British rearmament followed.

That Britain should be fully armed in a troubled world, to defend herself from any possible assault, has been a basic principle of British Union long before the National Government, which had criminally neglected our defences, consented to tardy and inefficient rearmament. Disarmament can only be won by world agreement which proportionately reduces the strength of all great nations and leaves the relative strength the same and the immunity from attack the greater. But armament by political parties which have grossly neglected the elementary duty of Government to put Britain in a position of self-defence, as part of an arms race which their blunders have precipitated is a very different matter. Arm we must if other nations are armed, but every effort of statesmanship should seek an end to the menace of arms race, which can only be achieved by world appeasement.

European Division and Eastern Anarchy

In the fatal sequence of events a divided Europe fell an easy and humiliated prey to Oriental anarchy. Germany isolated and encircled, like others in similar predicament, sought support where she could find it, and to the Berlin-Rome axis was added an understanding with Japan. As a result, in face of a divided Europe, Japan was able to cut loose in the Orient, with Great Britain an impotent and humiliated spectator.

A united Europe and a rational policy would at any time have averted the disaster by firm intimation to Japan that north of the Yangtze river, but no further, she was at liberty to do what Britain did in India, and in bringing order where anarchy and bloodshed ruled to find an outlet for her population and access to raw materials. Similarly the dignity and strength of a united Europe could have secured the relatively bloodless suppression of slave trading barbarity in Abyssinia and legitimate expansion for Italy, in full accord with the civilising mission which Britain herself undertook throughout the world. But Europe was divided, and from this division of the mind and spirit a sequence of catastrophe has arisen. Japan, forbidden to expand in Northern China, exploded throughout the Far East, and Italy, forbidden to expand where her legitimate interests were affected in the prevention of slave raiding from adjoining territory, exploded throughout the Near East. The simple lesson of history, and particularly of British history, is that great nations expand or explode. By denying expansion when no British interests were affected we have provoked explosion, and by encouraging to resistance primitive populations whom we had neither the will nor the means to defend, we sacrificed their blood and our own prestige.

We ask what British interest was served by long encouraging resistance to Japan in Northern China, except deference to our Governments Soviet ally, who required that territory as a breeding ground for Oriental Communism, and could exact support in the East against Japan in return for support in the West against Germany. Again we ask what British interest was served by partial and ineffective intervention in the Abyssinian dispute in deference to the clamour of international Socialism at the expense of British dignity and safety. The whole policy throughout has ignored reality. To ignore reality when heading for a precipice is to go over it, and to ignore facts when heading for a war is to incur war.

British Union Principles

So with the lesson in mind of past blunders, which we have consistently opposed, British Union policy in the foreign sphere rests on two principles: (1) to interfere in no quarrels which are not our concern. Britons shall fight for Britain only, and never again shall conscript armies leave these shores in foreign quarrel. Britain we will always defend from any attack, and we will provide the means for that defence, but never again shall British blood be spilt in an alien quarrel; (2) we will give leadership and make contribution to secure the material and spiritual union of Europe, on which alone world peace and British interest in world peace can rest. If, despite that leadership and contribution, the world in madness destroys itself by war we will "Mind Britain's Business" and thereby save our people from that catastrophe.

The New Germany

In that determination it is natural immediately to seek a solution of present difficulties with Germany and the establishment of friendship. That such a solution can be found is plain to anyone who has studied the facts of the new Europe and, therefore, understands the profound difference between the old and the new Germany. The Germany of the Kaiser rested on a system of export capitalism conducted by Judaic finance which challenged us on the markets of the world, and emphasised that challenge with naval rivalry that threatened our Empire. In historic survey the internal forces of that Germany, operating within the international system to which Britain was wedded, made a clash inevitable.

It is, therefore, important to realise that in 15 years of Hitler's struggle a new German psychology was created which rests on a conception exactly the opposite to that of the Kaiser. The new German does not desire a world wide Empire, for he believes that racial deterioration will result from such racial intercourse, and that the new German has another mission in the world than to elevate savages. These are reasons strange for the Englishman to understand, because he knows that the foremost achievements of his race have been evoked in the vast work of Empire building which, in the particular case of his Imperial genius, has led to no such deleterious results. But these facts are important in that they denote no longer a divergence but a community of objective. Britain requires in peace to develop her own Empire, and Germany desires in peace to incorporate within the Reich the Germans of Europe.

The desires of these two powers, therefore, for the first time become not antithetical but complementary. For a strong British Empire throughout the world can be regarded by the new German as a world bulwark against Oriental Communism, and a strong Germany in Europe can be regarded by the new Briton as a European bulwark against the same disruption that invades from the East the life of Western man. From new conceptions in Germany and in Britain can arise a new communion of interest to support the communion that should exist in a common blood.

France and European Solidarity

To this idea the writer, as a friend of the French people, is convinced that France can be attached once she, too, has won freedom from the vendettas of politicians and can be induced to realise that the legitimate expansion of Germany, in directions the opposite to any threat to French interest, is a strength to Europe, and, therefore, a strength to France in securing solidarity against the common menace that comes from the East. If this conception cannot be accepted by financial democratic Government in France it will at least soon arise from the chaos which financial democracy creates in that fair but unhappy country. For it must be admitted that a new sense has come to Germany, and no German in his senses will at infinite sacrifice make a bid to acquire overcrowded territory which belongs to France when his own people and relatively virgin soil summon him in the opposite direction.

Let us put ourselves for a moment in the German position and console ourselves and the French with the reflection that German affairs are no longer conducted by fools but by a man of singular intelligence. By recognition of the fact that the new German interests lie in the East rather than in the West of Europe, British Union does not mean that we seek joint action with Germany in the waging of war against Russia, although we shall forthwith break the present alliance with Russia. On the contrary, we seek peace with all countries, including Russia, and would only join with other powers in action against her if she menaced Great Britain and thus evoked our resolute principle of self-defence. But even the folly of Russian Communism will not challenge the might of an united Europe which, if need arose, would deal with her as easily as with a colonial expedition.

We seek not by war, but by the solidarity of the European spirit and plain commonsense, to secure that legitimate expansion of great nations which can avert the disaster of another and greater explosion. That solution will be found without bloodshed for the good and simple reason that none can resist a combination of the great powers of Europe. Britain, Germany, France and Italy have in this matter a basic community of interest which the victory of the modern movement in Britain can weld into an irrefragable instrument of action in the achievement of peace.

In foreign affairs, as in national life, the leadership principle prevails in reality, and Europe is lost without the united and effective leadership of the Great Powers. Too long we have suffered from the post war delusion that a tiny State, possessing a few thousands of backward population, was not only in theory but in practice the equal of a great nation with millions of advanced peoples to support material power and moral position.

Colonial Question

The great powers must unite and lead to peace, and this final blessing can only come from the victory of British Union in the land that is today the key to world peace. But, in giving leadership, Britain must also make contribution, and long before the colonial question was raised in acute and controversial form British Union declared willingness to hand back to Germany the mandated territories, on simple and clear conditions that they should not be used as naval or air bases against Britain, and that Britain might preserve such facilities as were necessary to her naval and air communications. Such a concession would present no difficulty to a Germany which has already accepted a 35 per cent ratio of our naval strength, and therefore made the maintenance of her potential colonial communications dependent on friendship with Britain. We will not surrender one inch of British territory to any power, but these colonies held in mandate from the League of Nations are not British in law, and in practice we are inhibited from their development for British purposes, with the result that territory, which in restoration would be an outlet and opportunity for Germany, is today a burden and expense to us. Yet the Conservatives, who have betrayed British Empire by throwing open British African possessions as the dumping ground of the world, are ready to jeopardise world peace in clinging to territory we do not require, while neglecting the territory which belongs to us at the expense of infinite sacrifice and heroism of virile generations of the British. So in passing it may be observed that once again the Tory proves himself not only a dog in the manger but also a fool.

Economic Peace

It is clear that the peace of the new world can only rest on material justice and to deny it is to court war. The access of Germany to raw materials and opportunity for outlet and expansion will solve the last material problem of the great powers, for the other dispossessed nations, such as Italy and Japan, have already found a solution by force that the financial democratic world with characteristic folly refused to reason.

Thus in the solution of the German problem it becomes possible for each great nation to build that comparatively self contained civilisation which is the surest guarantee of peace. To those who deny this elementary statement of fact we pose the simple question, what are modern wars about? The answer is clearly that modern wars are economic in the struggle for raw materials and for markets. Consequently if each great nation has access to raw materials, and opportunity to build a market in the purchasing power of their own people, the only effective cause of war in the world is eliminated. The urge to war will go with the suppression of the international struggle for raw materials and markets, and the financial parasite that inflames the fever. Then if the world goes to war the world will indeed be mad, because no reason can exist for war, and Britain with justice will have no part in that madness.

The New Europe

But in truth no such fear need exist, for the reason of the present malady of Europe is not so difficult to diagnose. It is a malady and division of the spirit, which transcends all material differences. Material justice must be done and the new world must be built on the sound reality of a fair economic basis. But deeper than every division of material things is the division of the spirit in the modern Europe. The old world and the new world are divided and they cannot mingle. Either the new world and the old world will collide in disaster or the new world will emerge as the final system of the modern age. Therefore on the fate of Britain depends the fate of mankind.

British Union advances with British policy, method and character suited to this nation and to no other. But we can understand those who in other countries have brought the new world to triumph by policy, method and character suited to their nations as no "democrat" ever can. Because, despite every divergence of policy and difference of national character, we have the same origin in the struggle of our betrayed generation of the war to redeem great nations from corruption, and in common with these others we have passed through the same ordeals and faced the same enemies. This origin of a common experience and determination that great peoples shall not perish from the earth gives us an understanding one of another and a sympathy in the mutual struggle with the dark enemy of mankind that the old world can neither comprehend nor disrupt.

We are British and before all else in our national creed we place Britain and our love of country, but because we love our land we can understand and work with those who love their land. Thus shall be born not only the material union but the spiritual union of the new world.

British Union

SO British Union emerges from the welter of parties and the chaos of the system. To meet an emergency no less menacing than 1914 because it is not so sudden or so universally apparent, British Union summons our people to no less an effort in no less a spirit. Gone in the demand of that hour was the clamour of faction and the strife of section that a great nation might unite to win salvation. A brotherhood of the British was born that in the strength of union was invincible and irresistible.

Today the nation faces a foe more dangerous because he dwells within, and a situation no less grave because to all it is not yet visible. We have been divided and we have been conquered because by division of the British alone we can be conquered. Class against class, faction against faction, party against party, interest against interest, man against man, and brother against brother has been the tactic of the warfare by which the British in the modern age for the first time in their history have been subdued. We have been defeated, too, at a moment in our history when the world was at our feet, because the heritage won for us by the heroism of our fathers affords to the genius of modern science, and the new and unprecedented triumph of the human mind, an opportunity of material achievement leading, through the gift of economic freedom, to a higher spiritual civilisation than mankind in the long story of the human race has yet witnessed. But for the moment the British are defeated and acquiescence in defeat means the end. On the one hand, continued lethargy can lead only to unlimited chaos, ending in ultimate destruction, and, on the other, new effort can open before us a vista of unparalleled and unlimited opportunity.

Humanity can never stand still, and at this moment more than any other in our history the alternatives before a great nation are heroism or oblivion. Can we recapture the union of 1914 and that rapturous dedication of the individual to a cause that transcends self and faction, or are we doomed to go down with the Empires of history in the chaos of usury and sectional greed? That is the question of the hour for which every factor and symptom of the current situation presses decision. Is it now possible by a supreme effort of the British spirit and the human will to arrest what in the light of all past history would appear to be the course of destiny itself? For we have reached the period, by every indication available to the intellect, at which each civilisation and Empire of the past has begun to traverse that downward path to the dust and ashes from which their glory never returned. Every fatal symptom of the past is present in the modern situation, from the uprooting of the people's contact with the soil to the development of usury and the rule of money power, accompanied by social decadence and vice that flaunts in the face or civilisation the doctrine of defeat and decline.

Above the European scene towers in menace Spengler's colossal contribution to modern thought which taught our new generation that a limit is set to the course of civilisations and Empires, and that the course that once is run is for ever closed. Every indication of decadence and decline which he observed as a precursor of the downfall of a civilisation is apparent in the modern scene, and from all history he deduced the sombre conclusion that the effort of "Faustian" man to renew his youth and to recapture the dawn of a civilisation must ever fail. History is on the side of the great philosopher and every sign of the period with fatal recurrence supports his view. His massive pessimism, supported by impressive armoury of fact, rises in challenge and in menace to our generation and our age. We take up that challenge with the radiant optimism born of man's achievements in the new realm of science that the philosopher understood less well than history, and born, above all, of our undying belief in the invincible spirit of that final product of the ages - the modern man.

We salute our great antagonist, from whose great warning we have learnt so much, but we reject utterly the fatality of his conclusion. We believe that modern man with the new genius of modern science within him and the inspiration of the modern spirit to guide him can find the answer to the historic fatality. But to ignore the evidence of the ages and to deride the contribution to human thought of Spengler's great intellect is appropriate only to the pallid "intellectuals" whose emasculated minds lack the energy to study his facts and the courage to face his conclusions. His facts stand, and the only relevant question is whether or not in this epoch of supreme scientific achievement man is armed with the weapons and possesses the will to challenge and to alter the very course of mortal destiny.

It is in immense answer to all past history of human fate that British Union emerges within British Empire and the modern creed in diverse form emerges in all great nations with the decisive challenge of the renaissance of the Western man. Underlying every difference in policy, method, form and character in different nations, the rise of the National Socialist and Fascist doctrine throughout Europe represents in historic determinism the supreme effort of modern man to challenge and overcome the human destiny which in every previous civilisation has ordained irretrievable downfall.

The doctrines of modem disintegration are classic in form and pervade the political parties, which fade from a flaccid and universal "Liberalism" into the sheer disruption and corruption of Socialism serving usury. The doctrinaires of the immediate past come to the aid of political defeatism with the negation of manhood and selfwill and the scientific formulation of surrender as a faith.

In the sphere of economics Marx portrays humanity as the helpless victim of material circumstance, and in the sphere of psychology Freud assists the doctrine of human defeatism with the teaching that selfwill and selfhelp are no longer of any avail, and that man is equally the helpless toy of childish and even pre-natal influence. Marx's "materialist conception of history" tells us that man has ever been moved by no higher instinct than the urge of his stomach, and Freud supports this teaching of man's spiritual futility with the lesson that man can never escape from the squalid misadventures of childhood.

By a fatal conjunction the materialist doctrines of these two Jews have dominated the modern "intellectual" world to the rout and destruction of every value of the spirit. This predestination of materialism has proved in practice even more destructive of the human will and spirit than the old and discredited "predestination of the soul." It has paralysed the intellectual world into the acceptance of surrender to circumstance as an article of faith. To these destructive doctrines of material defeatism our renaissant creed returns a determined answer.

To Marx we say it is true that if we observe the motive of a donkey in jumping a ditch we may discern a desire to consume a particularly luxuriant thistle that grows on the other side. On the other hand, if we observe a man jumping a ditch we may legitimately conclude that he possesses a different and possibly a higher motive.

To Freud we reply that if indeed man has no determination of his own will beyond the idle chances of childhood then every escape from heredity and environment, not only of genius, but of every determined spirit in history, is but a figment of historic imagination.

In answer to the fatalistic defeatism of the "intellectual" world our creed summons not only the whole of history as a witness to the power and motive force of the human spirit, but every evidence and tendency of recent science. Today the whole front of materialism is on the retreat and the scene of modern thought is dominated by the triumph of the spirit. In rout are the little men who taught that nothing could exist that they could not understand. Biology begins again to teach that the wilful determination of the species to rise above the limitations of material environment is the dominating factor in evolution.

In psychology the modern school declares that the conscious exertion of man's will prevails over the chance of heredity and environment. In physics the influence of the external to matter, the unknown, in short the spiritual provides phenomena for which the purely material can afford no explanation. In fact, every tendency of modern science assures us that in superb effort the human spirit can soar beyond the restraint of time and circumstance.

So man emerges for the final struggle of the ages the supreme and conscious master of his fate to surmount the destiny that has reduced former civilisations to oblivion even from the annals of time. He advances to the final ordeal armed with weapons of the modern mind that were lacking to the hand of any previous generation in the crisis of a civilisation.

The wonders of our new science afford him not only the means with which to conquer material environment in the ability to wrest wealth in abundance from nature, but, in the final unfolding of the scientific revelation, probably also the means of controlling even the physical rhythm of a civilisation. Man for the first time in human history carries to the crisis of his fate weapons with which he may conquer even destiny. But one compelling necessity remains that he shall win within himself the will to struggle and to conquer. Our creed and our Movement instill in man the heroic attitude to life because he needs heroism.

Our new Britons require the virility of the Elizabethan combined with the intellect and method of the modern technician. The age demands the radiance of the dawn to infuse the wonder of maturity. We need heroism not just for war, which is a mere stupidity, but heroism to sustain us through man's sublime attempt to wrestle with nature and to strive with destiny. To this high purpose we summon from the void of present circumstance the vast spirit of man's heroism. For this shall be the epic generation whose struggle and whose sacrifice shall decide whether man again shall know the dust or whether man at last shall grasp the stars.

We know the answer for we have felt this thing within us. In divine purpose the spirit of man rises above and beyond the welter of chaos and materialism to the conquest of a civilisation that shall be the sum and the glory of the travail of the ages. In that high fate *tomorrow we live.*

Oswald Mosley - May 1938

www.ingramcontent.com/pod-product-compliance
Lightning Source LLC
Chambersburg PA
CBHW061745270326
41928CB00011B/2385